The Navajos in 1705

The Navajos in 1705
Roque Madrid's
Campaign Journal

Edited, Annotated, and Translated by
Rick Hendricks and John P. Wilson

Foreword by David M. Brugge

University of New Mexico Press
Albuquerque

ISBN-13: 978-0-8263-1856-5

Frontispiece:
Old warrior with lance and shield in Keams Canyon,
Arizona, 1893. (Photograph by James Mooney, reproduced
by permission of the Smithsonian Institution,
Museum of American History.)

© 1996 by the University of New Mexico Press.
All rights reserved. First paperbound printing

Library of Congress Cataloging-in-Publication Data

The Navajos in 1705: Roque Madrid's campaign journal
edited and annotated, and translated by
Rick Hendricks and John P. Wilson—1st ed.
p. cm.
Text in English and Spanish.
Includes bibliographical references and index.
ISBN 0-8263-1856-8
1. Madrid, Roque, 1644–ca. 1723—Diaries.
2. Madrid, Roque, 1644–ca. 1723—Journeys—New Spain.
3. Navajo Indians—History—18th century—Sources.
4. Navajo Indians—Social life and customs.
5. New Spain—Description and travel

I. Hendricks, Rick, 1956–
II. Wilson, John P. (John Philip), 1935–
E99.N3M2976   1996
978.9'02—dc20   95-41728
CIP

Designed by Sue Niewiarowski
Maps drafted by Jerry L. Livingston

Contents

Illustrations / vii
Maps / ix
Foreword / xi
Preface / xv
Introduction / 1
The Journal / 13
The Spanish Journal / 39
The Route / 63
Conclusion / 89
Biographical Sketches / 101
Abbreviations / 129
Notes / 131
Works Cited / 159
Index / 169

Illustrations

Navajo warrior / frontispiece
1. A page from Roque Madrid's campaign journal / xvii
2. Petroglyph of mounted riders with hats and swords / 4
3. Rio Grande Valley at Pilar (Cieneguilla) / 14
4. Crane pictograph in Gobernador Canyon / 17
5. Mouth of the cañada where Captain Gutiérrez watered the horse herd / 22
6. The Laguna de San Joseph, in a hollow between two peaks / 23
7. The winding middle course of La Jara Canyon / 25
8. The north face of Santos Peak, scene of the assault on 12 August 1705 / 29
9. Bluff at the junction of Tapicito Creek and Cañon Largo, setting for the battle of 14 August 1705 / 32
10. Ojo de Nuestra Señora with its large rock, autumn 1972 / 36
11. Vallecitos, New Mexico, in the Sierra Florida Mountains / 41
12. Looking downstream along the Navajo River / 46
13. A spacious meadow; the campsite on the afternoon of 10 August / 48

Illustrations continued

14. La Jara Canyon, where Navajo cornfields lay / 50
15. Los Peñoles; Magdalena Butte and Santos Peak / 52
16. Ojo de Nuestra Señora, on Wheeler Survey atlas sheet / 60
17. The campsite of 9–10 August 1705 / 70
18. The Laguna de San Joseph, now a shallow marsh / 73
19. Staging point for the assault in La Jara Canyon / 77
20. Santos Peak and the canyon country beyond, from the western end of Magdalena Butte (summer 1972) / 78
21. On top of Santos Peak, rocks piled along the edge / 79
22. Pueblito ruin at LA 2298, on the bluff at the junction of Tapicito Creek and Cañon Largo / 85
23. Painting of José de Naranjo / 119

Maps

1. The Route of Roque Madrid's Campaign / 10–11
2. The Laguna de San Joseph / 72
3. The Dawn Assault Through La Jara Canyon / 75
4. Los Peñoles: Santos Peak and Magdalena Butte / 80
5. The Encounter at the Junction of
   Tapicito Creek and Cañon Largo / 83

Foreword

Ethnohistory has a long tradition in the Southwest, beginning before the name was even coined. Adolph F. Bandelier was perhaps the first practitioner of the combination of anthropology and history. His example of a scholar working alone in both disciplines set a pattern that was followed by many who came after. Ethnologists and archeologists did their own historical research, while historians who wrote of Indian history acquired most of their knowledge of the ways of their subjects from the documents they utilized and the published works of anthropologists. It is rare to find a truly collaborative work by an anthropologist and a historian, for even in the years of the Indian claims cases, specialists in the two disciplines regularly worked separately.

The present work is an exception to that rule and a very successful example of the rich rewards that cooperation can produce. Rick Hendricks, historian, and John P. Wilson, anthropologist, began work independently on the Navajo campaign journal of Roque Madrid, neither being aware that the other was interested in the document. When they eventually learned of the other's efforts, rather than competing to see who could bring his work out first, they joined forces; we are all the benefactors of their wisdom.

Spanish colonial campaigns generated much more paper than is generally recognized, including initial testimony and correspondence justifying hostilities, a call to arms, muster rolls, orders of the day, and a journal written in the field, along with journals or reports sometimes composed by leaders of detachments from the main body of troops, a final summary report, and entries in the service records of soldiers who took part. Additional documentation sometimes appears in letters evaluating the success of the campaign, a treaty, church records of prayers for success before and thanks after the undertaking, baptismal records of captives taken, burial records of participants who were killed or died in the field, and retrospective accounts by participants or others recorded years after the event. Even this list probably does not exhaust the possibilities, for a major portion of the Spanish Archives of New Mexico has been lost. Diligent search by both Hendricks and Wilson has added some scattered documents to round out our knowledge of the expedition itself, and a biographical sketch by Hendricks of each Hispanic participant who can be identified is also included. Beyond this the historical context is set forth clearly and gracefully.

The Spanish side of the war is but half of the story, of course, and it has taken considerable care on the part of the authors to present hints as to the Navajos' views, for no documents were created on their side, nor has any identifiable oral tradition survived the intervening three centuries since the war, of which this expedition was only a part. Wilson has, however, been able to identify archeological remains indicating Navajo occupation at various points along the route of the army, and he suggests locations for cornfields mentioned in the journal. Wilson's explorations to trace the route provide many questions with satisfying answers that I believe will stand the test of time.

The authors have exercised restraint in their interpretations of the data so as not to infer more than is justified. There are many puzzling bits of information in the document that raise as many questions as are settled and that will give scholars a great deal to think about for years to come. The publication of the Spanish text along with the translation greatly enhances the value of the work for further research, for often the Spanish usages contain hints and connotations that cannot be easily rendered in English, ample fodder for theorizing and speculations that go beyond the simple account of an army's march through Dinetah.

I not only await the publication so that I may make use of it as a source on Navajo history, but I also look forward to reading what uses other scholars, both Navajo and non-Navajo may make of it. I hope that all readers will be challenged to think as well as be engaged by this story.

David M. Brugge
Albuquerque, NM
December 1994

Preface

On the night of 10 August 1705, Mre. de campo Roque Madrid and his army rode in silence across the unfamiliar landscape of northern New Mexico. His captains were seasoned veterans, among the most experienced and capable fighting men in New Spain. The sun went down, and three hours later the moon, a three-day-old crescent, set as well. They continued westward in darkness, struggling through brambles and rocks but still undetected. Almost at dawn they found the first milpa, or field of maize, of the enemy. Everyone changed to fresh horses. Then they struck.

Our purpose is to present the campaign journal and tell the story of this army; where it came from and where it went, what happened to it, and what it accomplished. To do this has required a true collaborative effort between a historian and an archeologist. The historian (Hendricks) is an editor on the Vargas Project, whose central task is publication of the journals from Gov. Diego de Vargas's two terms as governor of New Mexico as well as records of his interim successor, don Pedro Rodríguez Cubero. These span the years 1691–1704. In 1982 John L. Kessell obtained for the Vargas Project a copy of a transcript of the campaign journal kept by Roque Madrid, one of Vargas's captains, during an expedition against the Navajo Indians in August 1705. Although this document was added to the Vargas Project files, the historian did not make immediate use of it.

Earlier the archeologist (Wilson) asked the historian for information pertaining to the career of Roque Madrid. This was not an idle interest, because he had been aware of the transcript of the journal since graduate-school days and finally obtained a copy in 1970, with the objective of eventually publishing it. He made a rough translation and began accumulating background information, while giving priority to field trips to work out the actual route.

While researching Adolph Bandelier's career as a documentary historian for a paper to be delivered at a 1990 conference celebrating the sesquicentennial of his birth, the historian ran across the transcript. He made his own translation, prepared a Spanish version employing modern orthography, and also did background research that focused on the identification of participants on the expedition.

In 1991 the historian remembered the archeologist's query about Roque Madrid, which led to an exchange of letters and the discovery that both of us had the journal. We quickly decided to combine our efforts to bring it to publication. This has been a wise decision and a fruitful collaboration, because each brought strengths to the project that otherwise would have been lacking. The published journal is placed in the context of its time and is firmly grounded in the geography of the country where the events took place.

This journal is the earliest eyewitness account from the old Navajo country. We give it in English translation and in the original Spanish, with only as much annotation as is needed to understand it. An appendix provides biographical information concerning those participants we have been able to identify. The journal is unusually literate and dramatic and has needed only minimal editing or explanations. It records the advance of a small

1 / Proceedings of 16 August 1705, folio 9v of Roque Madrid's campaign journal. (Sender Collection, Document 3, State Records Center and Archives, Santa Fe)

army composed of presidial soldiers, militia, and Pueblo Indian auxiliaries, from San Juan Pueblo through northwestern New Mexico to their eventual destination at Zia Pueblo, in the course of which these allies fought three battles with the Navajos.

We initially worked from the transcript that Adolph Bandelier's father made in 1889, during a visit to his son in Santa Fe. According to Bandelier's note, the original was then in the possession of don José Segura, whose father had retrieved it when the archives in Santa Fe were thrown out in 1870. Bandelier apparently never made use of the transcript, which is not particularly surprising since his interests lay with the Pueblo Indians. After a few years, he deposited this and other transcripts of Spanish documents in the Peabody Museum at Harvard University as the archives of the Hemenway Expedition, which had employed him. These transcripts are there now, in the Tozzer Library.

The original was lost to sight after 1889, but more than a century earlier fray Silvestre Vélez de Escalante had seen it in the archives at Santa Fe and quoted part of the entry for 11 August 1705 in his *Extracto de noticias*. This was published in part in 1856 and reprinted in 1962. In 1958 Frank Reeve published Father Vélez de Escalante's quotation in translation with some other incidental details, erroneously placing the events of 11 August at what he called Cebolleta Mountain, west of the Rio Puerco.[1] Reeve had no way of knowing the route of Roque Madrid's army either before or after its fight with the Navajos at what has proven to be Santos Peak, near Cereza Canyon in the Cañon Largo drainage. Frank McNitt published a summary account of the campaign based upon the rough translation editor Wilson loaned him.[2]

The location of the original journal was still unknown to us when we (still working from Bandelier's transcript) gave a joint paper on the campaign at the 1993 Historical Society of New

Mexico annual conference. Frank Wozniak was in the audience and told us afterward that a 1705 journal was in the Sender Collection at the New Mexico State Records Center and Archives in Santa Fe. The State of New Mexico had acquired the Sender Collection, a separate group of official records from the Spanish and Mexican periods in New Mexico, in 1984. Within a week Robert Torrez, state historian, furnished us a photocopy of this 1705 journal, which was indeed the one from Roque Madrid's August campaign. A letter-by-letter comparison of the original and Bandelier's transcript revealed only minor differences. Fortunately the original is complete. This and the journal from a brief foray in pursuit of Navajo raiders in April 1705 seem to be the only journals known to have survived from the Navajo expeditions of the eighteenth century.

The trail for us has been somewhat longer than Roque Madrid's, and at times more uncertain. After securing a copy of the transcript, Wilson focused upon reconstructing the route of the army. Some progress was made in 1971–73 during weekend trips. These resumed after 1975 and were continued at intervals through 1988. By that time only the portion between Tres Piedras and Chama, New Mexico, had not been worked out. In between trips there was time for the reflection and planning needed after a visit had shown that some proposed section of the route was impossible when checked on the ground. Two archeological sites, LA 2298 and LA 8948, were recorded in 1971–72 because of an intuitive idea that they had figured in the expedition. The really big break came in 1988 when the mystery of a key landmark, the Laguna de San Joseph, was finally solved. After that the course of travel through the country west of Chama fell into line, and in many places it was possible literally to walk in the company's footsteps. We hope that whoever works out the route from Tres Piedras to

Chama in detail will have as much enjoyment as we did in following the army through the Dinetah country, the traditional Navajo homeland.

As editors we have restricted our role to describing the condition of New Mexico in 1705, summarizing our current knowledge about early Navajo history, reconstructing the route of the expedition, and identifying some of the participants. We are cognizant of the fact that scholars might well have preferred a semipaleographic transcription of the original Spanish. Nevertheless, so that more readers can appreciate the uncommon beauty of the language, the Spanish conforms to modern orthography, except for a few instances, which are noted.

Because this is a campaign journal, the perspective is entirely that of the Spaniards and their allies. The Navajo voice is silent. Still there is no indication that the soldiers were disdainful of their foe, and by the standards of the time they conducted themselves normally and did what they were expected to do. Even the torturing of the two women would have been routine and is recounted matter-of-factly. The implied losses among the Navajos may have been exaggerated; only eight deaths were actually recorded, though Gov. Francisco Cuervo y Valdés later recalled the Navajo campaigns as uncommonly bloody. The army's rapid advance and orderly return, its extremely low losses in men and animals, and its perseverance with virtually no logistical support until a decisive engagement was won, show that Governor Cuervo y Valdés had fielded an experienced and disciplined force; literally his first team. Their uncertainty at times was due to a lack of familiarity with local geography.

The Navajos displayed outstanding courage and a good tactical sense. Whether their principal captain, Perlaja, was in overall charge of the defense we are not told, but it seems likely that he was. In La Jara Canyon the Navajos were surprised, but they rallied immediately to the bluffs above and left the Spaniards to burn their homes and destroy the milpas. There was little point in resisting this laying waste of the milpas, and at no time did they do so. After La Jara Canyon the army was under constant observation, and the Navajo leaders probably chose Santos Peak as the site to make their stand. It was a wise decision, and the Navajos fought hard there, achieving a tactical victory. After Roque Madrid moved on to the south, it was obvious to the Navajos watching that the army had only one way out and would have to pass under the bluff where the third encounter subsequently took place. There the Spaniards and their Pueblo allies gained the day by means of a stratagem, but as before the Navajo warriors fought with skill and determination.

This August campaign did not end the expeditions against the Navajos; indeed in September the New Mexicans did it all again, by a somewhat different route. The result was a relatively short-lived peace, followed by more campaigns. This journal gives us a first look into the old Navajo country, made more valuable because it is an eyewitness account and is not duplicated by any documents that have survived until more than a century afterward. It is a rare window into a previously obscure corner of New Mexico's history.

We wish to acknowledge the aid of several colleagues. The assistance of the New Mexico State University Astronomy Department in calculating the phase of the moon on the night of 10 August 1705 is much appreciated. Stephen Williams, now retired from the Department of Anthropology, Harvard University, and formerly director of the Peabody Museum there, obtained permission to publish their transcript of Roque Madrid's diary. Frank Wozniak's timely suggestion as to the location of the original document, which proved to be correct, was most welcome. Regge Wiseman recalled his 1975 survey along Muñoz Canyon, which may have been the first to discover early Dinetah Phase campsites. For his introduction to Navajo history many years ago and valued assistance since then, both in person and by his prolific publications, we are indebted to David M. Brugge. The late Frank McNitt, who may have been the only other person to see the transcript before 1991, was fascinated by it and strongly urged publication. We hope he would approve what we have done.

Introduction

Even before his arrival in Santa Fe to take up the post of interim governor of the province of New Mexico, Francisco Cuervo y Valdés knew he was in for a difficult time. As he journeyed north he was delayed in El Paso, which was besieged by marauding Apaches.[1] Soon after taking possession of the governorship in Santa Fe on 10 March 1705, Cuervo y Valdés set about an assessment of the situation of the colony.[2] He found the Navajos and the Gila, Chilmos, and Faraón Apaches in a state of war and immediately took steps to safeguard the province until campaigns could be launched.[3]

In the well–established tradition of New Mexico's colonial governors, Cuervo y Valdés blamed his two fractious, litigious predecessors, Diego de Vargas and Pedro Rodríguez Cubero, for what he described as deplorable civil and military conditions. This had become traditional as a new governor replaced an old one. By heaping abuse on the outgoing official, a newly arrived governor was in a better position to claim every success and make excuses for reverses.

On 18 March he held the first muster of the Santa Fe presidio. Soon he would formulate a request for an additional thirty men from New Biscay, but before he could put his reorganization of New Mexico's defense into motion, two groups of Navajos fell on the Tewa pueblos of San Ildefonso, Santa Clara, and San Juan. In response Cuervo y Valdés dispatched a twenty-five man squadron on a retaliatory foray to punish the enemy and recover stolen livestock. Because of the head start the Navajo raiders had and the weakened condition of the Spaniards' mounts, the expedition produced only frustration.[4]

Cuervo y Valdés then ordered a muster of able-bodied men capable of bearing arms in the three principal communities of northern New Mexico. Guns recently supplied them at crown expense were examined, as were available horses. The results gathered from Santa Fe, Santa Cruz, and Bernalillo were shocking.

The Santa Fe muster took place on 20 April 1705. Of the seventy-four men, among them many of New Mexico's leading citizens, only forty-eight had any weapons and most lacked items from the standard kit. Fifty-seven men had no horses or mules; a total of fifty-four animals were available. Almost none of the citizens had ammunition and most were poorly clothed.[5]

The situation revealed in Bernalillo on 22 April was far less grim. Twenty-seven of thirty-seven citizens were fully armed except for *cueras,* though without ammunition. There were sixty-five horses and mules on hand. By sharing remounts with their neighbors, the militiamen from Bernalillo could be ready to join an expedition with much less assistance from the governor.[6]

In Santa Cruz five days later, eighty-three potential militiamen turned out for the muster. If anything the state of preparedness there was worse than in the provincial capital. Sixty individuals had no horses or mules, nearly to a man they lacked some vital element of a fighting man's equipment, twenty-two had no weapon at all, and most were poorly clothed. Everyone needed a supply of ball and shot.[7]

One hundred ninety-four men had answered the call to arms, but the resulting ragtag militia was not fit to take the field.

Nevertheless Cuervo y Valdés took what steps he could. In April and May, the governor distributed gunpowder to the citizenry and established a cordon to protect the colony until conditions were more propitious to go on the offensive. Presidial troops were distributed at seven sites: Santa Fe, Acoma, Cochiti, Jemez, Laguna, Santa Clara, and Zuni.[8]

As it developed over time, Cuervo y Valdés's strategy was one of protecting the Pueblos against other Indian groups such as the Apaches and the Navajos, who, according to contemporary observers, had emerged as a serious problem in 1703, raiding from mountain rancherias in areas closest to Spanish occupation. Navajos carried out many thefts, invasions, and killings of Spaniards and Pueblo Indians.[9] By defending the Pueblos, Cuervo y Valdés consolidated the gains that Diego de Vargas had begun to implement by a policy of mutually beneficial alliance between the Spaniards and Pueblos against outside groups before his death in 1704.[10]

In order to solidify the defensive position and alleviate the hardships being suffered by the populace, Cuervo y Valdés sought to supply needed foodstuffs and livestock. He distributed maize left over from Vargas's administration and sent for six hundred horses and five hundred head of cattle from New Biscay. Clothing, tools, and additional food were ordered and presidial soldiers resupplied.[11] By June 1705, Cuervo y Valdés was ready to take the battle to the enemy. His first move was to the southwest, against the Gila Apaches.[12] Perhaps the initial choice was influenced by his rude greeting at El Paso. Whatever the case, by late summer he was ready to launch a major expedition against the Navajos, who had provided a similarly hostile welcome to the Santa Fe area.

If other eighteenth-century campaigns can be used as a guide, some fifty to sixty presidial soldiers, thirty to forty militiamen, and some three hundred Pueblo auxiliaries formed the typical

2 / *Petroglyphs of mounted riders wearing hats and wielding swords, in Crow Canyon, a tributary of Cañon Largo.*
(Photo courtesy of Dr. Hugh C. Rogers, Farmington, New Mexico.)

fighting force. During this period, it was not uncommon for sixty to seventy-five percent of an army to consist of Indian allies. The numerical superiority of the Pueblo auxiliaries over the Spaniards made it practically impossible for the former to be controlled by the latter. Therefore the Pueblos could seek retribution for depredations committed against them by the now common foe.[13]

Roque Madrid stated that he received 1 quintal of gunpowder and 2 quintals of lead molded into shot on 15 March 1705 from Cuervo y Valdés. He added that he had used them up on the first campaign, which he had carried out on the governor's orders, to the Navajo country with sixty-five men, both citizens and presidial soldiers, and on escort duty around Santa Clara and San Juan.[14] In the campaign journal, on several occasions, operations are conducted in which squadrons of one hundred Indian allies participated, indicating that as many as several hundred were available to complement the Spanish troops. Moreover the journal indicates that there were more than seven hundred horses on the campaign.[15] The muster of this expedition has not come to light. It was held on 31 July 1705 at San Juan de los Caballeros, after which Roque Madrid and his troops departed, the first Spanish force to penetrate the mountain fastness of Navajo country in twenty-seven years.

And what of their enemies? These were the Apaches de Navajo, now called the Navajos but referred to then most often as Apaches. Scholars have debated for a century as to when, where, and under what circumstances these southern Athapaskans entered the Southwest. The literature on their history is a large one, much of it drawn from the same body of early Spanish documents.[16] The argument is often whether the Navajos arrived late in the Southwest, perhaps around the time of the Coronado expedition, or if they had dwelt there prehistorically. In these contentions it is easy to forget that the documents are not first-hand descriptions but instead report what someone said or saw or alleged about the Navajos or their country. The generalities that can be drawn are much less useful than direct observations, such as those a campaign journal would record.

Until now the earliest contemporary, eyewitness accounts of visits to the Dinetah, the traditional homeland of the early Navajos in northwestern New Mexico, have been from the early nineteenth century. A partial exception might be the testimony of witnesses and refugees who had campaigned or lived among the Navajos.[17] We can only wish that these visitors had told us more. Some information can be gleaned from the scant records of the short-lived effort at missionization of the Navajos that the Franciscans undertook in the 1740s.[18] In addition there are the more specialized studies of references to Puebloan refugees among the Navajos as a result of rebellions in 1694, 1696, or other times,[19] and of Navajo traditions about captives and refugees who lived among them and gave rise to new clans.[20]

The historical reviews have been quite thorough, and there is no need to repeat them. In recent years the majority view on the time of arrival has been that the Navajos came late,[21] in part because convincing evidence for their presence prehistorically has been lacking. How to resolve this question one way or the other has been the problem, and documents cannot provide much help.

Archeology was called upon as early as 1912 to shed light on the early history of the Navajos.[22] This line of inquiry has generated its own body of literature. One branch has focused upon the *pueblitos,* or small stone houses, of the Dinetah country.[23] Seventeen or more of these sites have tree-ring dates, and, with the exception of site LA 2298, these dates have clustered in the early and middle eighteenth century. Since there is no evidence that pueblitos predate A.D. 1700 by more than a few years if at all, we have historical references to the Navajos that are earlier than their pueblitos.

Pueblitos seem to have enjoyed only a few decades of popularity. Our best evidence on their origin and use is from the testimony of a dozen witnesses before New Mexico Gov. Joaquín Codallos y Rabal, in 1745. All of the men had entered Navajo country as members of expeditions at various times between 1705 and 1743. Eleven of the witnesses said in effect (quoting from the response of Pedro Sánchez) that "they [the Navajos] live on the tops of the mesas in little houses of stone. And that the reason for their living in those mountains is because the Yutas [Utes] and Comanches make war upon them."[24] Roque Madrid made no mention of these stone houses in 1705, but the *torreones* he attacked on a return foray in 1714 were probably early pueblitos.[25] Periodic hostilities with the neighboring Utes in what are now Colorado and Utah remained a problem for the Navajos through the middle nineteenth century.[26]

As far back as the 1940s, claims were made about other Navajo sites in northwestern New Mexico having tree-ring dates in the late sixteenth and seventeenth centuries. With the exception of site CM-35, on Chacra Mesa, these sites cannot now be identified.[27] Site CM-35 is a fortified Mesa Verde pueblo on an isolated knoll, whose 1350vv to 1598++vv range of dates probably represents a short occupation by Pueblo refugees from the Spanish assault on Acoma in February 1599, or by natives fleeing the hunger and privations elsewhere in New Mexico at that time.[28]

During the 1950s archeological research in the Navajo Reservoir district of northwestern New Mexico resulted in the description of a Dinetah Phase, dated from about A.D. 1500–1700 and intended to encompass the earliest Navajo manifestations in the upper San Juan River drainage.[29] That project found very few sites from the period. The concept of the Dinetah Phase fell into relative disuse and remained so until the mid-1980s.

The findings from a decade of contract research have now given us a profusion of reports on Dinetah Phase sites that lie within and north of the traditional Navajo homeland. South of the San Juan River and along Gallegos Canyon, two midden locations, one with two hearths, yielded radiocarbon dates from the late A.D. 1400s. At two sites above Blanco Wash, excavations in the brush and log structures, hearths, and other features of the Dinetah components provided late fifteenth-century to early sixteenth-century C14 dates, as well as one much earlier. Two shallow structures and associated hearths at the San Juan Breaks site south of Farmington, New Mexico, gave three radiocarbon dates centered in the early to middle fifteenth century.[30] Small camps with Navajo and Jemez black-on-white pottery have been reported along Muñoz Canyon,[31] and many others are recorded in the New Mexico ARMS data base.[32] Several have been found in southern Colorado.[33]

North of the San Juan and east of the La Plata River, within 2 miles of the Colorado border, at least thirty-five small, Dinetah Phase sites were discovered during the surveys for a coal mine. Seven excavated sites there yielded the remains of brush structures and forked-pole hogans, hearths, pits, and middens. A total of seventy-nine dates were derived from radiocarbon samples, obsidian-hydration, and thermoluminescent analysis of pottery sherds. These dates ranged from approximately A.D. 1350 to 1700, with the majority centered in the sixteenth and seventeenth centuries.[34] One site, LA 61838, has produced tree-ring dates of 1455vv, 1464vv, 1490vv and 1560vv.[35]

The chronological position of these La Plata Valley sites in particular makes the conclusions of two pioneers in Navajo history seem almost prescient. Washington Matthews's calculations, based upon legendary testimony, carried the beginnings of the Navajo Nation back to A.D. 1200 to 1400. Frederick Webb Hodge revised the same evidence in the light of historic factors and arrived at a date of about A.D. 1485.[36] Their methods may seem arcane, but their results may warrant another look.

Our study is not an archeological one, and it is not proposed to review all of the recent, intensive research that bears on the early Navajos. The implications of this research are only now being worked out. For example, contacts with the New Mexico pueblos appear to have been very limited, as shown by the paucity of material items, and the influence of the latter accordingly small. As for the entry of the Athapaskans into the Southwest, the best support is now for an intermontane or Rocky Mountain route rather than by a hypothetical southern movement along the western border of the High Plains.[37] One very interesting finding has been a lowering of the beginning date for an important Navajo pottery type, Gobernador Polychrome, to at least the mid-1600s.[38]

What has happened is that archeological findings in the past few years have broken down many of the older strictures. The evidence is now overwhelming that ancestral Navajos were present along the New Mexico–Colorado border and for an unknown distance south by A.D. 1500 and possibly a century and a half earlier. These people made pottery, dwelt in hogans and brush shelters, and were agricultural to some extent. From the writings of fray Gerónimo de Zárate Salmerón, we know that the Utes were living above the Navajos by the 1620s.[39] To extend a theory that correlates archeology and linguistic differentiation among the Numic groups, which includes the Utes, perhaps it was the eastward expansion by their ancestors that by A.D. 1600 forced the early Navajos south of the San Juan River.[40]

To this rapidly expanding archeological picture we can now add an unparalled historical view of the early Navajos, from the little-known journal of a Spanish military expedition that claimed it was the first to penetrate the Navajo heartland. This was certainly the first force from outside since the Pueblo Revolt of 1680, and the journal has much of the freshness and descriptive detail found in the first written records from a new country. The Spaniards and the Navajos were already well acquainted; they had known one another for a century or so, often as adversaries, which might explain why details about the Navajos themselves are slight. This aside, the journal is a vivid account in its own right. By reconstructing its route carefully, we can show where and when various episodes took place. At present it stands as the earliest eyewitness account of the Navajos and their homeland in northwestern New Mexico.

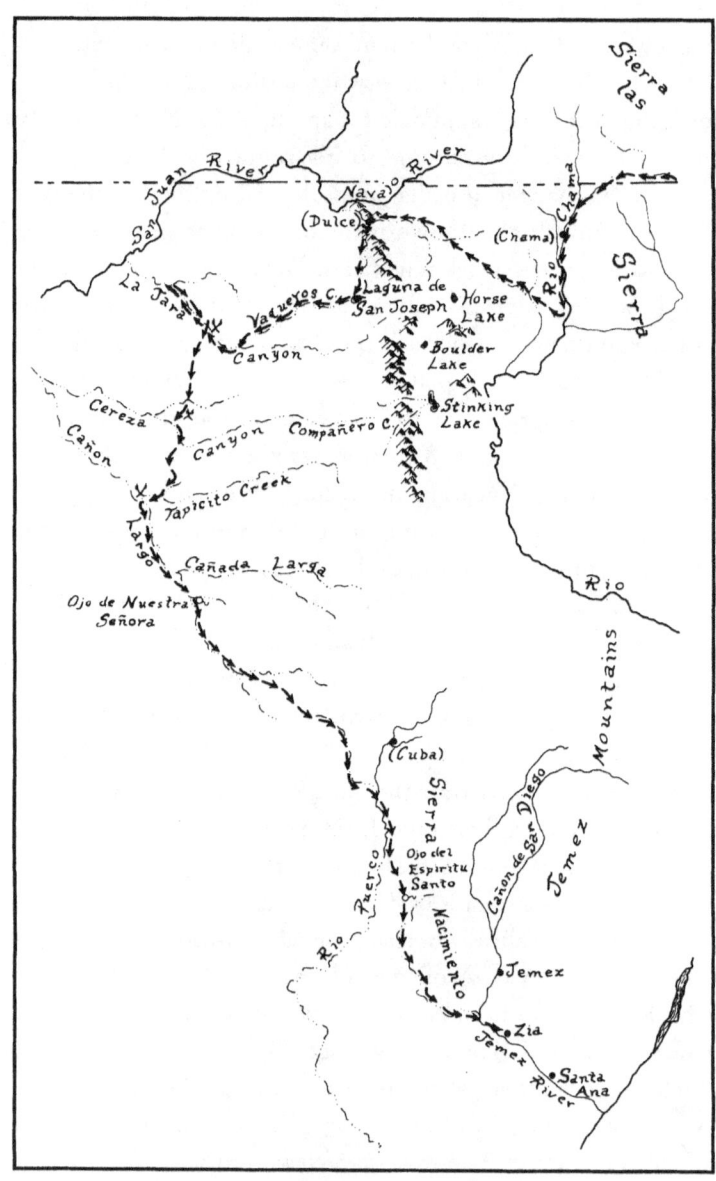

Map 1
The Route of Roque Madrid's Campaign

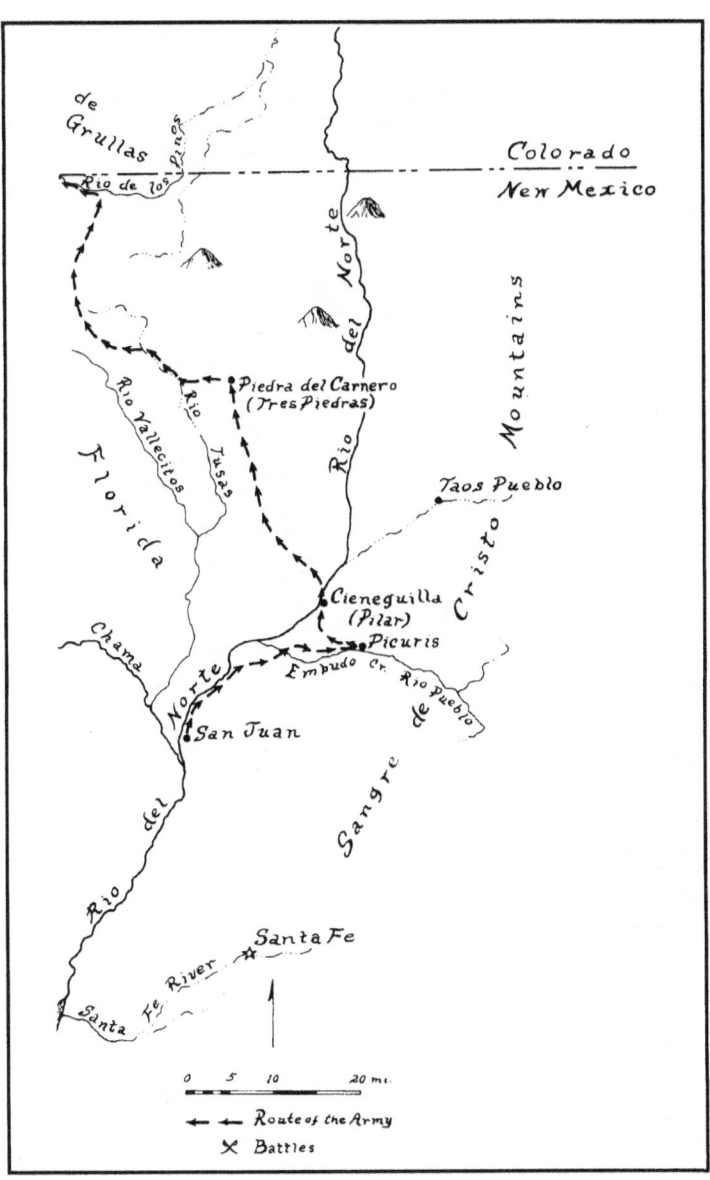

The Journal

In this pueblo of San Juan de los Caballeros, on 31 July 1705, I, Maestre de Campo and principal military leader Roque Madrid, by order of the lord governor and captain general, don Francisco Cuervo y Valdés, knight of the Order of Santiago and treasurer and factor of the Royal Treasury office of the city of Guadalajara, go forth to make war by fire and sword on the Apache Navajo enemy nation.

To comply with what I was ordered, I was obliged to hold a muster to examine the Spanish and Indian weapons. I did this on said day, month, and year. Lt. general don Juan de Ulibarrí was present, and after holding muster, which was much to my satisfaction, he handed the troops over to me. I took the route to the Río del Norte and halted my company along its pleasant banks, near El Embudo.

On 1 August of said year, I left the banks of the river for the pueblo of the Picuris. Along the way, sixteen Indians from Tesuque Pueblo joined my company. I halted my company one-fourth of a league from the pueblo, having traveled just over 5 leagues that day.

On the second day of said month and year, I set off, marching with my company, struggling through a land of very difficult terrain because of the many rocks and woods. Arriving at a spring called La Cieneguilla, I learned that the reverend father chaplain

3 / Rio Grande Valley at Pilar (Cieneguilla, New Mexico). The army after leaving Picuris Pueblo came from this direction on 2 August 1705. Looking south, summer 1972.

was awaiting me there. He had been appointed chaplain of my company by the very reverend father vice-custos, Father fray Francisco Jiménez, who is in charge of the mission of the pueblo of San Gerónimo de Taos.

I ordered my company to march ahead and went to see the reverend father. Forty Indians of the Taos nation joined us at that place, whereupon I examined their weapons, because they had not passed muster in the *plaza de armas*. I found them to be adequate, for which I was thankful, and took the route of my company in order to overtake them. I joined them in the gorge, on the banks of the Río del Norte. We crossed it with great difficulty and manifest risk to our lives, which God was pleased not to endanger. Once the whole company had crossed, I set up camp on a narrow bank with much tanglebush and little pasture, because there was no more suitable place to halt. I traveled 6 leagues that day.

On the third of said month and year, my company departed, traveling with much greater difficulty up the gorge in a northerly direction, to a point where it was necessary for all the mounted squadron to dismount. This was in order to lead the horses through the difficult terrain and because of the steepness of the climb. I continued in the direction of the campsite called Piedra del Carnero. I halted there and set up my camp, at a distance of 10 leagues from the river gorge.

The fourth day of said month and year, we set out from the campsite of Piedra del Carnero, marching west along a pleasant cañada with abundant pasture until we arrived at the middle of the mountain range. I gave it the name Sierra Florida because of the diversity of flowers there and because it is less rugged and mountainous. There are several streams fed by rain showers and heavy dew. I halted my company on the banks of a shallow river whose current flows south to a well-pastured and spacious valley, where that night a frost fell upon us. That day I traveled 6 leagues.

On the fifth of said month and year, we set forth from the campsite of the Sierra Florida and its river, still traveling in the same westerly direction. I halted at a broad, scattered bordering fringe at the foot of the mountain range. There is abundant good pasture. I traveled a short journey that day, because the Indians who were knowledgeable about that land told me there was no water up ahead, except at a great distance from this campsite, which I named Nuestra Señora de Covadonga.[1] I traveled 3 leagues that day. I halted my company beside the river of the Sierra Florida.

That same day I sent the war captains from the Tewa and Picuris nations, who knew those mountain ranges and woodlands, to reconnoiter a route where Spanish arms had not been for some thirty years.[2] The captains returned from their patrol on the sixth of the present month.

As soon as they arrived at this camp and in my presence, they laid before me as many difficulties and inconveniences as they possibly could. The least was to say that if we continued, we would lose all the horses, and it would be well to give thanks to God if we were each able to leave on the horse we were riding. That was how bad the woods were, with fallen logs, sharp rocks, and ravines. They told me they were telling the truth and that I would not complain about them after I had seen it with my own eyes.

The seventh of that month and year, despite the information the war captains gave me, I decided to follow the slope and the breaks of the mountains by a route no Spaniard or person from any other nation had taken until now. First, however, I took the precaution of doubling the squadrons for the horses, so that with everyone's help, they could be driven without any losses. I took the lead, invoking Nuestra Señora de la Conquista to open the way for me to be able to ascend such heights.

After I had traveled a short distance, the woods were so thick that inside them, the day became as night. Yet, God saw fit that after a little more than one-fourth of a league, I came out to a country that was somewhat easier of passage, with much pasture and beautiful partridges, which were as large as a Castilian hen.[3] After having traveled about 4 leagues to the north, I came out in a valley that was not too large, with excellent grazing and many cienegas and springs. I named it the Valle de Santiago. There are

4 / Crane pictograph in Gobernador Canyon.
(Photo courtesy of Dr. Hugh C. Rogers, Farmington, New Mexico.)

two cañadas very close to one another and two small creeks that flow to the east. They are very difficult places, and much work was required to cross them. I set up camp after having traveled 6 leagues that day. Immediately after having established it, I sent the war captains from all the nations to reconnoiter to see whether they could find a path or road so that I could continue on my way. From this Valle de Santiago, you can see the Sierra de las Grullas and hear the cranes' call.[4]

On the eighth of said month and year, after the allies arrived from their patrol, they returned to me and raised even greater objections to my entrada. I paid them no heed, because my mind was made up to continue until I saw everything to its conclusion. I immediately ordered the horses rounded up and continued on ahead, still traveling in front of the Sierra de las Grullas, through the middle of a forest so thick and close that the animals got stuck. They could go neither forward nor backward. For this reason, I ordered the campaign captain, Juan Roque Gutiérrez, to take charge of herding and getting the horses out. This he did with great solicitude, frequently dismounting to aid his companions. Everyone did this in short order with the greatest effort and many falls and tumbles. This was why Alejo Gutiérrez and Juan de Zamora broke their *escopetas,* and many others were bent and damaged.[5] For this reason, I took the precaution of giving two pistols to those who broke their weapons.

In these woods and mountains are many creeks with clear waters. I arrived at the eminence of the loftiest peak of Las Grullas and its river. There I took a fall down the mountain with the horse I was riding. Only by a miracle from La Conquistadora did I escape with my life.[6] The Río de las Grullas runs west to east, splitting two eminent peaks with gentle, cool waters containing many trout.

I crossed to the other side and the cañada, where God saw fit to better the road in some respects. Having first traveled through 6 leagues of steep mountains, I arrived at a splendid shoreline at the banks of the river. There I established my camp and immediately sent the scouts to reconnoiter to see whether they could spot fires or the enemies' tracks. I ordered them not to build fires in the camp so that neither the smoke nor the fire would be seen at night. Every care was taken with the sentries and watches of the camp. Capt. Juan Roque Gutiérrez saw to this with zeal and vigilance.

On the ninth of the said month and year, I marched with my company toward the Chama River, through a forest of tall pines by an easy and pleasant road. About 5 leagues to the south, I arrived at a spacious, pleasant valley with many cottonwoods and good pasture, by the banks of the aforementioned river. The current is very crystalline and not turbulent as it flows into the Río del Norte. I quartered there to await the scouts I had sent out the day before. They arrived after our chaplain had celebrated the Holy Sacrifice of the Mass. The previous day he had preached an inspiring sermon, motivating the soldiers to treat the enemy justly. Because for this it was necessary for them to be in God's grace, in no way did he excuse himself from the task of hearing confessions from all those who wanted to prepare themselves and enter into battle in a state of grace. He was ready to disregard any risk when the time came.

The scouts arrived, saying that they had seen neither enemy fires nor tracks and that the search for them could continue safely. At this point a controversy arose between the *genízaros*[7] of the Jemez nation and Dirucaca, the Jemez saying that we should head straight ahead for Los Peñoles. Dirucaca and Pamuje, an Indian of the Tewa nation,[8] said that we should enter by the Río Grande, which was where the most defiant Apaches were camped. In this way we could take all the enemy from the rear. They would be careless, since no Spaniards had entered that country before. We would come out near the headwaters of the Río Grande. In this way we could not help but have successful battles by entering through the middle of the Apache country, which was what we were looking for in order to punish their daring. Hearing this opinion, I decided to go toward the Río Grande, despite the objections the genízaros from Jemez brought up to me about the vastness of the land and its rugged nature.

I departed, continuing my journey toward the Río Grande. After the company had traveled about half a league, the men in the vanguard, who were in a wide cañada that descends from the mountains, spotted two forms. They overtook them and found them to be Indian women, one with her son on her back. One was a Christian from the Jemez nation and the other an Apache. I immediately separated them, putting them to torture so that they would tell me where they were from, what they were doing there, or where their camps were.

They responded that about three months ago, because of the rigors of hunger, they had departed Navajo to look for quelites in this area to feed themselves and their husbands. The latter had gone hunting that day up in the mountains, and the Indian women had come down to look for quelites to eat. They did not know whether their husbands would return, because they had wounded a deer the day before and had gone to look for it. They gave me no information about other people or rancherias, even on pain of death, because they did not know anything.

Based on my experience, I realized that being able to capture the males was uncertain, and I did not want to delay my journey waiting for them. Thus I left, traveling south. In about two and one-half leagues, I arrived at the waterhole that is in a cañada near some crags. The water tastes very bad and is fetid. The scouts who always precede the company caught up with me there. They told me they had seen nothing, not even tracks.

Thus, I continued, still traveling through very rugged mountains and *embudos*. After I had traveled about 5 leagues north, the embudo and cañada became so closed that it was necessary to climb up to the crest of the mountain range. We did this with great effort because of its height and the malpais. First we had to cross a small arroyo and a very marshy swamp. I halted on the summit of the mountain range to wait for the rest of the company and horses to make their way up. At that time, we saw two fresh tracks. I feared lest they be from scouts for an ambush and that in those brambles they might achieve a surprise.

Because everything was already up, I continued on this route in the direction of the Río Grande. After a short distance, I stopped my men in a cañada of a small, highly obstructed creek. There was so much tanglebush that the horses could not drink that day, in which I traveled a little more than 10 leagues.

On the tenth of said month and year, Capt. Juan Roque Gutiérrez set out for the Río Grande to water the horses. At a distance of one-fourth of a league from the campsite where the company was stopped, there is a river with a little less water than the Río del Norte when it is low. It is lined by many chokecherries and manzanillas and flows west, at the foot of a high mountain range. The captain returned from watering the horses; immediately and without delay, I tried to leave, taking every measure necessary to launch a dawn raid on the milpas and first rancherias, which the map indicated were now close by. As always, I sent scouts ahead.

We were traveling through a very pleasant cañada until we arrived at the foot of the mountain range. There we found tracks

5 / Mouth of the cañada where Capt. Juan Roque Gutiérrez watered the horse herd on the morning of 10 August. Looking south across the Navajo River.

of the Apache Indians who carefully patrolled their land. These were the ones whose tracks we had seen the day before. We knew that they had seen us, because they had painted some crosses in the road and a line that crossed the road. By this sign they meant we were friends and thus we should not cross over the line.[9]

I called together the war captains of all the nations and told them that, after taking every precaution, the captains should follow these tracks with a squadron of soldiers and the map, which was the principal guide of all my company. The Apaches had not spotted us; even though they had painted the crosses, it was because they were timidly awaiting our weapons and knew neither where we were coming from nor when. They were being very careless, and little by little this was becoming apparent in their tracks. Yet if the captains followed them, the Apaches would already be out of the mountains and could see them. If any escaped, they would warn their rancherias. For that reason, I withdrew the above order and set off, traveling along the cañada until arriving at the foot of the mountain, which we climbed with some effort.

6 / The Laguna de San Joseph, "in a hollow between two peaks." The laguna lay in the loop formed by the modern roads.

From its heights we could see a laguna in the middle of the mountain range in a hollow between two peaks, all surrounded by somewhat swampy land, its water slightly salty. Outside the laguna is a small spring of very good water. At a distance of about a harquebus shot from the south shore is a spacious meadow with abundant pasture. I stopped my company there because the map said that the way out of the mountains was very near. We stayed here until late afternoon so they could not see our trail dust. At this campsite, our chaplain distributed a *carga*[10] of *pinole*[11] among my soldiers, because he saw they were lacking provisions.

At five in the afternoon, I left the Laguna de San Joseph, so named by me because I was the first to go there. I traveled the rest of the day and until around midnight[12] along some low, heavily wooded hills until I spotted a fire that I imagined was made by the Apaches who were up ahead. I halted and sent a squadron of soldiers with some Indian allies, all on foot, to surround and grab them in order to have a more certain guide. They had been gone for three hours when they returned to where I was. They found nothing more than the fire itself. I started off again from there and after about 1 league, entered the most indomitable land encountered so far, consisting of rocks, tanglebush, and arroyos. It continued until I arrived at the first milpa of the Apaches of the Río Grande, where I called a halt.

Everyone changed to fresh mounts in order to launch the dawn assault, which took place on the eleventh of said month and year. I left the vanguard squadron together with that of the horse herd and some Indians with the pack train and their people's burdens. I ordered the cavalry leader to march, following me with the whole company, because there was no suitable place to stop.

After taking these measures, invoking the name of our lord Santiago,[13] I went on to launch the dawn assault throughout the

7 / *The winding middle course of La Jara Canyon, looking south from a bench partway up the eastern side.*

cañada, which was more than 4 leagues in extent. I found all the *ranchos* and houses abandoned.[14] I found only two warriors who were killed climbing up the mesa. Likewise two Indian women died at the hands of the Indian allies, without my being able to prevent it. We caught one young boy.

I rejoined my troops. After we laid waste to their milpas and burned their houses, the Apaches came out on top of the mesas to shout at us, without our being able to hurt them, because there was no way up. I reached my company, which I found destroying the milpas that they had left behind and burning the ranchos. The Indian allies were looting the household goods that [the Apaches] had taken up on the mesa. They took a mare and her colt.

There the cavalry leader, Miguel de Herrera, told me that while the horses were passing through a gap, the Apaches had shot two of them with arrows from the heights of the mesa. The enemy achieved nothing more, because the squadron leader and his companions immediately went to their defense with their weapons, until the horses passed the narrows. My company delayed for a time while the men took some refreshment, which was ears of tender maize, since that was all there was.

I set off, marching for Los Peñoles toward the south, where I climbed a mesa of very difficult terrain. To be able to do so free of the enemy, I posted the men on both flanks. The vanguard had climbed up first, along with a hundred Indian allies. I remained with the rear guard until the horses had gone up, with great difficulty. As soon as all my company and the horses were up, I again gave over disposition of the troops to Capt. Juan Roque Gutiérrez and departed, taking every measure necessary to launch a dawn assault against Los Peñoles and their rancherias.[15] While traveling, I came upon some rancherias before reaching Los Peñoles. There we killed an Apache, and another escaped to the mesa above with several wounds. We captured a young boy, but the Indian allies could not overtake the wounded fugitive, because they were fatigued from thirst and exhaustion from having covered more than 8 leagues over various mesas.

Continuing my route toward Los Peñoles, making assaults and destroying milpas, I found the Indians about to kill an old woman and stopped them. She then fervently requested the water of baptism. She was baptized, and then they killed her. They captured another woman with her daughter. I continued assailing them until arriving at Los Peñoles, where I found all the people up on top.

All my companions and I were very disconsolate and afflicted to see the horses staggering and dizzy from thirst. There was neither remedy for this difficult situation nor any way to punish the enemy. They were making great fun of us, spying from the heights of Los Peñoles. Thus, it was that our horses went among the rocks sniffing and neighing in such a way that it seemed that they understood and were asking God for water with their cries. In the midst of this affliction, our chaplain began to clamor to Heaven, asking for relief; all my companions and I joined him. Our exclamations reached Heaven, and suddenly a small cloud arose giving a little rain, but it was not even enough to wet our cloaks.

Shortly the squadron leader, Mateo Trujillo, began to shout that the horses should be taken down to be watered at a dry arroyo we had passed earlier, because it was flowing like a great flood. We praised God, thanking Him for this miracle. Then He sent rain in such abundance that all the fields turned into lagunas. In the hour and a half that the rain lasted, the water gave us no place to halt. In the meantime, the cavalry was destroying milpas.

When the rain stopped, we spotted some sheep at the foot of the *peñol*. Because the soldiers thought there were many, they rushed off to Los Peñoles to catch them for food. There turned out to be only two.

The Apaches' having requested peace terms with great shouts was the occasion for silencing the weapons that day. We agreed that the following day we would talk and make peace. They knew very well that we were coming, four days before I arrived, because a young boy from Bernalillo of their nation had come to them and given them the information that soon the Spaniards were coming to make war on them. This was why I had found people so wary and hidden in the cañada of the Río Grande. The same was true for all the Navajo country. They did not want to fight but to be our friends.

At this we retired to the camp, which was very near the peñol, taking the greatest care possible that they not achieve some surprise, fearing the treachery of these barbarians because of my many years of experience fighting them.

From the Laguna de San Joseph to Los Peñoles was 16 leagues, all over rough terrain of embudos, mountain ranges, and very mountainous cañadas, such that in the darkness of the previous night, six horses were lost. In all that distance, there is no water at all.

A short while after the cavalry solders had finished the night watch, the enemy attacked violently, screaming very loudly. I left the camp in such good time that the men at arms and I had time to catch the horses and charge the enemy, driving them into retreat to the woods and the foot of their peñol. Though we called them through the Indian interpreter to come down and fight, they did not want to. They told me that when the sun came up we would fight, that the people were united to have done with us, that the horses were many and the Spaniards few, and that we would not get a single horse out. God Our Lord saw fit for us to meet the dawn on the twelfth with nothing at hand.

At sunrise, as they had said, an even larger number of Indians attacked the troops from ambush. At that time I sallied forth to meet them with most of my Spaniards and Indian allies, leaving the rest in camp with the horses, which I kept within sight. With this precaution, I gave the Santiago, and all the soldiers and Indian allies advanced and attacked with such forcefulness that the enemy immediately tried to turn tail and flee to their peñol. Our men wounded many of them during their retreat, because the ascent up their peñol was narrow, by way of a ladder left there, which soon caused them to be pressed by our weapons. As they blocked each other's way up, some misstepped and fell, dying before their people's eyes; they saw them dragged away and scalped.[16]

I tried hard to take their peñol and its ascent to dislodge them, but I could do no more than get to the ladder. They concentrated their force there, throwing and rolling rocks down. Realizing that it was impossible to take their peñol; that one could not fall back

8 / *The north face of Santos Peak, scene of the assault on Los Peñoles, 12 August 1705.*

from there without risking the soldiers; that in doing this, two companions and three Indians were wounded; and that this was wasting ammunition without any gain, I tried to withdraw.

I did so very slowly, getting down to my troops and leaving the enemy wailing and very confused from seeing their companions dead. I stayed in this campsite for about two hours, so that the enemy would not think I was taking flight. I then set off, marching, and went to establish my camp one-half league from Los Peñoles. All the way I destroyed milpas. God saw fit that day for it to rain a copious downpour that was sufficient to water all the horses, whose number surpassed seven hundred, including those of the Indian allies. As soon as the downpour and destruction of the milpas ceased, I went out to sleep without water, near a mesa.

There the Indians began to shout that they wanted peace and to be our friends. That night they carried off two horses and killed another that returned to them.

On the thirteenth of said month and year, I departed for a spring that the genízaros told me had sufficient water for my horses. Marching along, I spotted some tracks and immediately sent the campaign captain with two squadrons of soldiers and a hundred Indian allies to reconnoiter to see whether they were scouts for some ambush or whether some rancheria was on the move. In either case, they were to make war on them. As soon as I gave this order, I continued my journey to the spring. When I arrived there, it was greatly disappointing to me. Not only was there not enough for the horses, but the men consumed it as soon as they arrived. This land is so sterile and dry that it seems it has not rained in ten years.

I left my troops in this outpost and went along the arroyo for more than 2 leagues, to see if there was any water dammed up or any pools. Not finding any, I returned to the troops and found the horses in the same difficult situation as the day I arrived at Los Peñoles. This deeply saddened me, and I did not fail to take action. I left again, trusting in God and His Most Holy Mother that they would succor me in this time of need.

Having traveled upstream toward the aforesaid arroyo about 1 league, I stumbled upon my relief in a wide cañada with water and pastureland, filled with many clusters of milpas, all appropriate to our purpose. I returned to my troops, very pleased, giving them this good news, at which they all rejoiced and gave thanks to God.

I went forward to the cañada to await Capt. Juan Roque Gutiérrez and the allies who had accompanied him. In my presence, he reported to me everything that had happened and that he had seen. He had been laying waste to milpas, when the enemy fell on him to drive the men away from there. He closed so tightly with them that they soon fled. Many from the mesas followed them. The same occurred with the men who were mounted. They took from atop a peñol some thirty sheep and rams that they brought back dead to the camp and divided among the allies and soldiers. He further reported that up the cañada there were abundant pools with water and many milpas in other cañadas. That day I traveled 4 leagues through cañadas and difficult terrain.

On the fourteenth of said month and year, I devised a ruse for the Apaches. To accomplish this, I advised a hundred Indian warriors from all nations that while the troops were leaving, they should climb the mesa under cover. I encouraged them sufficiently to do this and ordered them that when they found the enemy, they should take them by fire and sword. I also advised them that as soon as I halted my company, I would go to the tip of the mesa with a few soldiers to divert the enemy's attention, talking to them while the allies managed to get close to and behind them. This was so that both of us at the same time could give them the punishment they have so deserved.

As soon as I halted my company, I departed for the mesa with two squadrons of soldiers and some of the Indian allies. Immediately after I arrived, the Apaches began to shout, saying that they wanted to do us no harm, that they wanted peace, and that for this reason we should talk at length. I kept it up and prolonged the conversation, gaining time so that my aim might be achieved. The parley reached the point where they decided that two Indians should come down and that I should send two to the foot of the mesa. One who went was Naranjo and the other the governor of Zia Pueblo. This was done so that they could embrace each other. I assisted them with all these plans, which would further the achievement of my aim. I ordered Naranjo and the governor that, when our people raised a cry above, they should each em-

9 / *Bluff at the junction of Tapicito Creek and Cañon Largo; setting for the battle of 14 August 1705. The LA 2298 pueblito is on top of the bluff.*

brace their man and kill him. For this reason, they each took the precaution of carrying a concealed knife. Behind them another two climbed down, and I sent another two of mine. One was Juan Griego and the other, the war captain. They were under the same orders that I gave the others who had climbed up.

They parleyed for a long time, and during all this, without the slightest sound from our men, the negotiations reached the point where two Indians came down to the bottom of the hill on foot to embrace and talk with me. This parley lasted more than two hours; I was still diverting their attention when it began to rain. They took their leave and climbed up. The reason I let them out of my grasp was because we knew nothing of our men up there. At the exact instant that they took their leave of me, having climbed the first bench of the mesa, our men appeared on its summit. They had just been spotted by a scout the enemy had posted. The Apaches quickly took flight, and our men chased after them. Those from above and below, the soldiers and Indians, and ten soldiers and I went to secure their escape route and the way down, so none of the enemy could escape.

Two who attacked in this direction died at our hands and the rest above, by lance and bullet wounds. Of the more than thirty that were there, no more than five escaped, not counting two who in a great fury threw themselves over the edge, or the many more deaths that the Indian allies will have carried out among the women and *chusma*[17] over the distance they covered on top of the mesa. This is their custom, and no matter how much I reproach them, they neither take heed nor pay attention unless Spaniards are present.

When this battle was over, I retired to lay waste to milpas. In the meantime, all the men came down. As soon as they had arrived, they reported to me that as the Indian allies were going along the mesa top, an Apache joined them without knowing who they were. According to him, their fear of our weapons made them terrified. They caught and bound him, in order to bring him before me.

When asked where he was headed, he answered that he was going to see the lord governor. As those with this prisoner were returning, they came to the edge of a cliff, where he hurled himself over the steep precipice with great fury.[18] Because the person who was bringing him bound did not let go of the rope, he went over with him. I withdrew my company to settle down and rest from what had transpired, thanking God that in the whole battle only one of my men was lost, and he was an Indian.

On the fifteenth of said month and year, I remained in this campsite of Nuestra Señora de Guadalupe. I so named it because I found a print of her image, which the reverend father fray Agustín de Colina had sent to the captains of this area by way of an old Apache woman.

I spent the day finishing the destruction of their milpas, sending squadrons along various cañadas and mesas to reconnoiter the land. They returned and reported to me that they had seen neither Apaches nor anyone else. Everything was silent, as if no such people existed in the world. As I was coming from laying [the land] waste in a cañada very near the mountain range, my companions spotted a little Indian boy. They did not find any tracks other than his. From this I reasoned that out of fear they even gave their children up for lost, judging from how skinny and ill the boy was. All this occurred in lands never before seen by Spaniards until I discovered them.

Proceedings of 16 August 1705

In this campsite of Nuestra Señora de Guadalupe, on the sixteenth of said month and year, I, the maestre de campo and principal military leader of the men at arms who are in this campsite making war by fire and sword against the heathen enemy of the Apache nation: We have given them the exemplary punishment deserved by the daring, robberies, and killings they have perpetrated against us in breaking the peace that they maintained for ten years. This is of record in these war proceedings.

I have seen how beset and fearful they are. In the period of three days that I have stayed in this campsite, several times various squadrons have gone out to reconnoiter the land through different embudos, mesas, and cañadas, territory that our weapons have never entered before. We can neither catch nor find anyone, not even their tracks, because they are so careful. They have placed their hideout far from our company. They are not daring and have not made smoke signals on their higher elevations.

I felt that it was appropriate to call a war council of the active officials, military leaders, and reserves. This was so that with everyone's opinion, we could decide what was most appropriate to the service of both majesties, a soldier's honor, and the fulfillment of my duty. I asked them whether it was appropriate to continue on or withdraw their weapons to their royal presidio.

I am giving an account of everything to my governor and captain general, who will decide and take the most appropriate measures for the future. I also asked them if it was appropriate to continue the return to the Río Grande. There is no relief either from the hardship or the hunger we suffer.

They all responded to the same end: That if it were advisable to continue to see what we could do to inflict the most damage on the enemy, it would be well to continue, even though with much difficulty; but the enemy would always be hiding and retreating from where they could be hurt, because of the fear they have developed of our weapons during the advances we have made against them.

At present the men find it impossible to punish them more than we have done up to this point. This has been done without losses on our part, rather with great success in everything. They therefore think it appropriate to withdraw our forces to their royal presidio. In the meantime, the enemy may drop the vigilance it presently maintains. Then, if at that time they do not go around groveling, asking to make peace (now I understand why, at the campsite of the spring we call Nuestra Señora, near a large rock, they put fourteen crosses marked in the ground and other signs of

10 / *Ojo de Nuestra Señora (now the Otero Ranch Spring) with its large rock, autumn 1972. Much of this area has been drained since 1972, and the vegetation is accordingly reduced.*

peace for us),[19] we could make war on them again with greater advantages than at present, because all the men are now experienced in this land, the ways in and out, and we would return with more food. It is of record that many of the soldiers are ill from not eating anything but ears of tender maize. Even these are all gone. As great servants of his majesty and as Catholics, they feel they should withdraw their weapons. They signed this so that it will be of record for all time.

I, Maestre de campo Roque Madrid, recognized as right and well founded the arguments expressed in their opinions; I find them appropriate to the service of both majesties. I share the same opinion as all the others. We should withdraw our weapons from this country until another time.

I am signing these proceedings with my secretary of war, Juan Roque Gutiérrez [rubrica]
Joseph Domínguez [rubrica]
Tomás Holguín [rubrica]
Cristóbal de Arellano [rubrica]
Miguel de Herrera [rubrica]
Martín García [rubrica]
Mateo Trujillo [rubrica]
Cristóbal Serna [rubrica]
José de Naranjo [rubrica]
Roque Madrid [rubrica]
Before me, Sec. of War, don Antonio Castrillón [rubrica]

On the sixteenth of said month and year, I set out, marching on the return to my royal presidio. That day I traveled to the south, finishing laying waste to the milpas along the way without a sign of the enemy, seeing neither smoke nor tracks of those frightened individuals who survived the punishment related in these proceedings. Having traveled about 6 leagues, I arrived at the spring of Nuestra Señora, where I set up camp and spent the night.

On the seventeenth, it was reported to me that there were milpas and rancherias very near this campsite. They belonged to the people at peace in the pueblos of Laguna and Acoma. For this reason, I did not take up our weapons against them, so they might know that the Spaniards only make war against their enemies and keep safe those who say they are not.

I set off that day, still marching south with my company. I traveled through cañadas and rough terrain until I arrived at a cañada with many pools of water. I halted there and sent Capt. Juan Roque

Gutiérrez to make a brief report to the lord governor and captain general about everything. That day I traveled 6 leagues.

I departed from this campsite on the eighteenth day of said month and year. I traveled in the same direction, until I arrived at the Espíritu Santo spring. Nothing worth writing about happened. That day I traveled 7 leagues.

On the nineteenth of said month and year, I left the spring for Zia Pueblo, where I quartered with my troops. I traveled 7 leagues that day. From this pueblo, which is the first of this Christian nation, I passed with the troops into the presence of the governor and captain general so that, having seen this report and these war proceedings, his lordship might decide what was most appropriate. So that it may be of record, I signed it in that pueblo with my secretary of war on 20 August 1705.

Roque Madrid [rubrica]

Before me, Sec. of War don Antonio Alvarez Castrillón [rubrica]

The Spanish Journal

En este pueblo de San Juan de los Caballeros en treinta y un día del mes de julio del año de mil setecientos y cinco, yo el Maestre de Campo Roque de la Madrid, cabo y caudillo principal que de orden del Señor Gobernador y Capitán General don Francisco Cuervo y Valdés caballero del Orden del Señor Santiago, tesorero factor de la Real Caja de la ciudad de Guadalajara pasa hacerle la guerra a sangre y fuego a los enemigos de nación apache navajo.

Y para cumplimiento de las órdenes que en mi obtengo, me precisa el pasar muestra para reconocer las armas así españolas como indias, lo cual se hizo en dicho día mes y año hallándose a ella el teniente general don Juan de Ulibarrí quien después de haber la dicha muestra muy a mi satisfacción me entregó el campo, cogiendo la derrota al Río del Norte. Paré mi campo en sus amenas riberas cerca del embudo.

El día primero de agosto del dicho año salí de la playa de dicho río para el pueblo de Picurís. En el camino se incorporaron con mi campo diez y seis indios del pueblo de Tesuque. Y fui a parar mi real distante un cuarto de legua de dicho pueblo habiendo andado este día poco más de cinco leguas.

El día dos del dicho mes y año salí marchando con mi campo por lo encumbrado de una tierra de muy peñoso camino por las muchas piedras y monte que en ella hay. Y llegado a un ojo de agua llamado La Cieneguilla tuve razón que en dicho puesto me aguardaba el Reverendo Padre Capellán nombrado por el muy reverendo Padre Vice-Custodio para capellán de dicho mi campo, que tiene a su cargo la misión del pueblo de San Gerónimo de los Taos, el Padre fray Francisco Jiménez, adonde dí orden fuese marchando el campo y me fui a ver con su Paternidad Reverenda, incorporándose en dicho puesto los indios de la nación taos, siendo su número cuarenta, adonde reconocí sus armas por no haber pasado los dichos muestra en la plaza de armas, las cuales las hallé suficientes se lo agradecí, cogiendo la derrota de mi real en su alcance e incorporándome en el en la caja y orillas del río del norte vadeándolo con crecido trabajo y riesgo manifiesto de nuestras vidas, lo cual fue Dios servido no peligrase nada y así que hubo pasado todo el campo senté el real en una playa angosta de bastante greña y poco pasto por no haber otra parte más cómoda para poder pararlo. Caminé este día seis leguas.

El día tres del dicho mes y año salió mi campo con crecidísimo trabajo caminando la caja arriba hacia el norte adonde fue necesario que la escuadra que iba de caballada se desmontase toda para poder arrear la caballada por la maleza de la tierra y lo áspero de su subida, llevando siempre el rumbo al paraje llamado la Piedra del Carnero distante de la caja del río diez leguas adonde hice alto y senté mi real.

El día cuatro del dicho mes y año salimos del paraje de Piedra del Carnero marchando hacia el poniente, por una cañada muy amena y de mucho pasto hasta llegar al centro de la sierra, la cual le puse la Tierra[1] Florida por las diversas flores que en ella hay y lo poco áspero y montuosa que es con diversas corrientes de aguas llovedizas y muchos rocíos que en ella caen. Paré mi real a orilla de un corto río cuya corriente lleva al sur muy empastada su tierra y extendido valle adonde esta noche nos cayó una helada. Caminé este día seis leguas.

11 / The valley at Vallecitos, New Mexico, in the Sierra Florida Mountains, summer 1972.

El día cinco del dicho mes y año salimos del paraje de la Sierra Florida y su río, caminando siempre con la misma derrota del poniente y fui a parar a un ruedo muy esparcido y ancho que hace a la falda de la sierra con mucho pasto y bueno. Anduve este día jornada corta por decirme los indios prácticos de la tierra no haber en lo de adelante agua sino era muy distante de este paraje por mí nombrado Nuestra Señora de Covadonga. Anduve este día tres leguas. Paré mi campo en el mismo río de la Sierra Florida.

El dicho día envié a recorrer la tierra a los capitanes de la guerra de nación teguas y picurís capaces de acuestas sierras y montes a reconocer la entrada por adonde habrá cosa de treinta años que entraron las armas españolas, los cuales dichos capitanes volvieron de la correduría el día seis del corriente.

Y luego que llegaron a este campo y mi presencia llegaron poniéndome los mayores imposibles e inconvenientes que decir se pueden pues el menos era el decir que si prosigíamos habíamos de perder totalmente la caballada que a buen negociar daríamos gracias a Dios de salir cada uno en el caballo que iba por lo espésimo del monte y palos caídos, peñasquería y barrancos, diciéndome que ya me decían la verdad que después no me quejase de ellos en viéndolo ocularmente.

El día siete del dicho mes y año sin embargo de las noticias que me dieron los capitanes de la guerra, resolví de coger la decaída de la sierra y sus deshechos por camino no andado de ningún español hasta estos tiempos ni de otra nación ninguna, dando primero la providencia de la dobla de las escuadras a la caballada para que con ayuda de todos pudiesen arrear sin pérdida alguna. Cogí la guía y punta, invocando a Nuestra Conquistadora para que me abriese camino para poder subir de dicha aspereza.

Y a poco andar era tan espeso el monte que a poco andar dentro de él se me oscureció el día, más fue Dios servido que a poco más de un cuarto de legua salí a tierra algo andable y de mucho pasto y hermosas perdices tan grandes como una gallina de Castilla y como cosa de cuatro leguas que hube andado caminando al norte salí a un valle no muy grande de muchísimo pasto, ciénagas y ojos de agua, al cual le puse el Valle de Santiago. Bajan por dos cañadas muy inmediatas la una a la otra dos cortos arroyos que corren al oriente, muy atascadores que para pasar es necesario hacerlo con mucho trabajo. Senté mi real después de haber andado este día seis leguas y luego que lo planté envié a reconocer a los capitanes de la guerra de todas naciones a ver si se descubría senda o camino para poder proseguir mi derrota. Desde este Valle de Santiago se divisa y ve la Sierra de las Grullas y se oyen sus cantos.

El día ocho del dicho mes y año habiendo llegado la gente amiga de su correduría me volvieron de nuevo a poner mayores inconvenientes para mi entrada de lo cual no hice caso por tener hecho el ánimo a proseguir hasta ver el fin de todo y luego mandé arrimaran la caballada. Y fui prosiguiendo siempre a la frente de la Sierra de las Grullas por medio de un monte tan espeso y de tanta palizada que se quedaban las bestias estacadas que ni atrás ni adelante podían andar, por cuya ocasión dí orden al capitán de campaña Juan Roque Gutiérrez llevase a su cargo el arreo y salida de caballada quien lo cumplió con mucha solicitud, desmontádose en muchas partes a ayudar a sus campañeros que lo hicieron todos muy puntualmente con grandísimos trabajos caídas y rodadas siendo esto causa de que Alejo Gutiérrez y Juan de la Mora quebraran sus escopetas sin muchas que se entortaron y maltrataron y para esto dí la providencia de dos pistolas a los dichos que se les quebraron sus armas.

Hay en este monte y sierra diversos arroyos con distintas corrientes. Llegué a la eminencia del altísimo Peñasco de las Grullas y a su río adonde me sucedió rodar por la sierra abajo con el caballo en que iba montado que solo por milagro de La Conquistadora pude escapar con la vida. Sale este Río de las Grullas de poniente a oriente dividiendo dos eminentísimos peñascos aguas muy suaves y frescas y con muchas truchas.

Pasé lo de la otra banda y cañada adonde fue Dios servido mejora el camino en alguna manera. Habiendo andado primero más de seis leguas de aspereza y serranía llegué a una espléndida playa a orillas del dicho río adonde planté mi real y luego despaché las espías a reconocer si divisaban lumbres o ver si rastros de los enemigos, dando allí orden que no se hiciesen lumbres en el real porque no viesen los humos o divisasen dicha lumbre de noche, poniendo todo cuidado en las velas y rondas de real, a lo cual asistió con todo esmero el capitán Juan Roque Gutiérrez con toda vigilancia.

El día nueve del dicho mes y año salí marchando con mi campo para el Río de Chama por un monte de pinos altos, andable y ameno camino; como cinco leguas al sur llegué a un valle espacioso y ameno de mucha alameda y buenos pastos a orilla del dicho río cuya corriente es muy cristalina no turbia como desemboca al Río del Norte adonde me alojé a aguardar las espías que había despachado el día antes, las cuales vinieron después de haber celebrado el Santo Sacrificio de la Misa nuestro capellán habiéndonos hecho el día antes una plática de gran doctrina animando a la gente de guerra a la ejecución recta contra el enemigo y que para esto era necesario fuese en gracia del Altísimo, que no se excusaba de ninguna manera al trabajo de confesar a todos los que quisiesen disponerse y entrar en la batalla en gracia que estaba pronto para no mirar riesgo ninguno en llegando la ocasión precisa.

Llegaron las espías diciendo que de ninguna manera habían visto lumbres ni rastros del enemigo y que así bien podía ir prosiguiendo en su busca. Aquí hubo controversia entre los genízaros de nación jémez y Dirucaca diciendo los de Jémez entrase derecho a Los Peñoles y Dirucaca y Pamuje, indio de nación teguas, que entrase por el Río Grande que era adonde estaba rancheada la apachería más rebelde, cogiéndoles las espaldas a todos los enemigos que estarían con descuido por no haber en ningún tiempo entrado españoles a dicha tierra, que iríamos a salir cerca del nacimiento del Río Grande y que de esta suerte no podíamos dejar de tener buenas funciones por entrar por medio de toda la apachería que era lo que buscábamos para castigar su osadía. Y con este parecer determiné el entrar por el Río Grande sin embargo de los inconvenientes que me propusieron los genízaros jémez de lo dilatado de la tierra y su aspereza.

Salí prosiguiendo mi viaje para el Río Grande y habiendo caminado el real cosa de media legua la gente de la vanguardia en una cañada ancha que baja de la sierra divisaron dos bultos, los cuales dieron en su alcance y hallaron ser indias cada una, una con su hijo a cuestas, una de nación jémez cristiana y la otra apache a las cuales luego dividí, poniéndolas en cuestión de tormento para que me declararan de donde eran, que hacían allí o donde estaban sus rancherías.

A lo cual me respondieron que había cosa de tres meses que con el rigor del hambre se habían retirado de Navajo a buscar yerbas por estas partes para mantenerse con sus maridos que habían ido a cazar este día la sierra arriba y que ellas bajaban a buscar quelites para comer, que no sabían si volverían sus maridos por ocasión de haber jareado un día antes un venado y lo habían ido a buscar, que de otra gente ni rancherías no me daban razón ninguna por no saberlo aunque les quitase la vida.

Y reconocido por la experiencia que me asiste lo incierto que estaba el poder cogerlos varones, no quise atrasar mi jornada con su espera y así fui caminando para el sur y como cosa de dos leguas y media llegué a aguaje que está en una cañada cerca de unos peñascos de muy mal sabor el agua y hedionda adonde me toparon las espías que iban siempre por delante del campo, los cuales me dijeron no haber divisado nada ni visto rastros.

Y así fui caminando siempre por sierras y embudos de bastante aspereza y como cosa de cinco leguas que hube caminado para el norte, se cerró tanto el embudo y cañada que fue necesario subir la eminencia de la sierra, lo cual se hizo con muchísimo trabajo por su altura y malpaís habiendo primero de pasar un arroyo pequeño y de mucho pantano. Hizo alto en la cumbre de la sierra a aguardar subiese todo el real y la caballada, ocasión de haber visto ya dos rastros frescos, temiendo no fuesen algunas espías de alguna emboscada y en aquella maleza lograra algún descuido.

12 / Looking downstream along the Navajo River where it "flows west, at the foot of a high sierra." The viewpoint is a ridge above the bridge north of Dulce, New Mexico.

Ya que estuvo todo arriba proseguí la derrota que lleva para el Río Grande y a poco andar paré mi gente en una cañada de un pequeño arroyo muy atascador de mucha greña que no podía ni pudo beber la caballada este día el cual anduve poco más de diez leguas.

El día diez del dicho mes y año salió el capitán Juan Roque Gutiérrez a dar agua al Río Grande a la caballada que distaba del paraje donde estaba parado el real un cuarto de legua. Es un río que lleva poco menos agua que el río del norte cuando está bajo, de mucha arboleda de capulíes y manzanillas; corre al poniente al pie de una alta sierra. Volvió dicho capitán de dar agua a la dicha caballada y luego sin dilatarme nada traté de salir a toda diligencia a dar albazo a las milpas y primeras rancherías que el mapa me dijo estaban ya inmediatas, enviando siempre por delante las espías.

Fuimos caminando por una cañada muy amena hasta llegar al pie de la sierra adonde hallamos rastro de los indios apaches que con cuidado corrían su tierra, que fueron estos los que el día antes habíamos visto su huella por lo que se da a entender de habernos visto por unas cruces que pintaron en el camino y una raya que cruzaba el camino en que daban a entender con esta seña que éramos amigos y así que no cruzasemos adelante.

Llamé a los capitanes de la guerra de todas naciones a los cuales les dije que luego a toda diligencia salieran tras estos rastros con una escuadra de señores soldados los cuales capitanes y el mapa que era la guía principal de todo mi campo, que no éramos sentidos de estos apaches que aunque habían pintado las cruces era por estar tímidos esperando nuestras armas y no saber por donde habían de entrar esa era la ocasión y que iban ellos con mucho descuido y poco a poco que lo reconocían en el rastro y que de ir tras de ellos ya estarían fuera de la sierra y podían divisarlos y si escapaba alguna irá a dar aviso a sus rancherías. Por lo cual razón detuve la orden de arriba y fui caminando por dicha cañada hasta llegar al pie de la sierra que subimos con algún trabajo.

Y desde su altura se divisa una laguna que está en el centro de dicha sierra en un recodo de dos peñascos toda rodeada de tule, algo pantanosa no muy salada su agua. Fuera de la laguna está un pequeño ojo de agua muy suave. Como un tiro de arcabuz de distancia hace en su orilla de la parte del sur una capaz vega con mucho pasto adonde paré mi campo por decirme la guía que ya

13 / "A spacious meadow with abundant pasturage," the army's campsite on the afternoon of 10 August. This meadow now lies just west of the junction between the highways NM 537 and US 64.

estaba muy cerca la salida de la sierra y que así paramos aquí hasta que fuese tarde y no viesen nuestro polvo. En este paraje repartió nuestro capellán a mis soldados una carga de pinole porque los veía faltos de bastimento.

A las cinco de la tarde salí de la Laguna de San Joseph[2] por mi puesta por ser el primero que ha llegado a ella. Caminé lo restante del día ya hasta cerca de medianoche por unas lomas bajas y de mucho monte hasta divisar una lumbre que discurrí ser de los apaches que venían delante; hice alto y despaché una escuadra de soldados con algunos indios amigos todos a pie que los cercaran y a mano los cogieran para tener logro de tener guía más cierta, los cuales fueron y a rato de tres horas llegaron adonde yo estaba y no hallaron más que la lumbre sola. Volví a salir de allí y a cosa de una legua entré por la tierra más indómita que hay en todo lo atrás andado de peñasquería, greña y arroyos hasta llegar a la primera milpa de los apaches del Río Grande adonde hice alto.

Y remudaron todos para dar el albazo que vino a ser el día once del dicho mes y año, dejando la escuadra de vanguardia con la de la caballada y algunos indios con el tren y cargas de los suyos y orden al cabo de escuadra de la caballada que fueran marchando en mi seguimiento con todo el real por no haber parte al propósito adonde poder pararlo.

Y después de haber dado estas providencias en nombre del Señor Santiago, proseguí comenzando el albazo por toda una cañada de milpas más de cuatro leguas, hallando todos los ranchos y casas despoblados, hallando solo dos gandules, los cuales murieron subiendo la mesa arriba. También a manos de los indios amigos murieron dos indias sin poderlo yo remediar y se cogió un muchacho.

Volví a incorporarme con mi real después de haberles talado sus milpas y quemado sus casas; salían a gritar en lo alto de las mesas sin poder ser ofendidos de nosotros por no tener subida alguna para poderlo hacer. Llegue a mi campo el cual hallé talando las milpas que habían quedado atrás quemando los ranchos y a los indios amigos saqueando los trastes que habían subido a la mesa y se les quitó una yegua con su cría.

Adonde me dió razón el cabo de caballada Miguel de Herrera que al pasar por una angostura desde lo alto de la mesa habían jareado dos caballos, que no lograron los enemigos más por acudir luego al reparo con las armas el dicho cabo y sus compañeros hasta que pasó la caballada dicha angostura. Detuve un rato mi campo mientras tomaba la gente algún refresco el cual fue de elotes por no haber otra cosa.

14 / Looking up La Jara Canyon, with its looping streamcourse. The Navajo milpas, or cornfields, destroyed by the army on 11 August 1705, lay along here.

Y luego salí marchando para Los Peñoles al sur adonde subí una mesa de muy mala tierra y para poderlo hacer libremente del enemigo tendí la gente por ambos lados habiendo subido primero la vanguardia y cien indios amigos arriba, quedándome yo en la retaguardia hasta que subió con grandísimo trabajo la caballada y luego así que estuvo arriba todo mi campo y caballada volví a dejar el real a la disposición del capitán Juan Roque Gutiérrez partiendo yo a toda diligencia a dar albazo a Los Peñoles y sus rancherías y yendo caminando dí en unas rancherías que están antes de llegar a Los Peñoles adonde se mató un apache y otro que escapó la mesa arriba con cuatro heridas y se les aprisionó un muchacho y los Indios amigos no pudieron alcanzar al fugitivo herido por lo fatigados que estaban de sed y cansancio de haber corrido más de ocho leguas por diferentes mesas.

 Y siguiendo mi derrota a Los Peñoles dando albazos y talando milpas hallé a los indios matando a una vieja. Detúvelos y luego pidió el agua del bautismo; con mucho fervor se bautizó y luego la mataron y se les aprisionó otra con su hija. Proseguí en mis albazos hasta llegar a Los Peñoles adonde hallé la gente toda arriba.

 Y yo y todos los compañeros con bastantes desconsuelo y aflicción de ver la caballada ya borracha y atarantada de sed y sin ningún remedio para aliviar esta pena como el poder castigar al enemigo que hacía gran mofa de nosotros divisando desde la altura de Los Peñoles de la suerte que andaba nuestra caballada entre las peñas oliendo y relinchando que parecía que entendían y pedían a Dios el agua a gritos y en medio de esta aflicción comenzó nuestro capellán a clamorear al cielo pidiendo el remedio y yo en su compañía y todos los compañeros cuyas exclamaciones llegaron al cielo y de improviso se levantó una pequeña nube que llovió muy poco pues ni aun los capotes se mojaron.

 Y a breve rato comenzó a gritar el cabo de escuadra Mateo Trujillo que bajasen la caballada al agua a un arroyo que poco antes habíamos pasado seco que venía con una grande avenida. Alabamos a Dios dándole gracias de este milagro y después nos la envió en tanta abundancia que todos estos campos se hicieron lagunas no dándonos lugar el agua en más de hora y media que duró a poder parar y en este ínterin estuvo la caballada talando milpas.

 Y así que sosegó el agua, se divisó en la falda del peñol unas ovejas, que juzgando la gente de guerra ser mucha se arrojó a Los Peñoles a quitarlas para su alimento y hallaron no ser más de dos.

15 / Los Peñoles: Magdalena Butte and Santos Peak, from the north.

Y a los apaches pidiendo las paces a grandes gritos que fue ocasión de que se detuvieran las armas aqueste día, quedando asentado el que otro día hablaríamos y asentaríamos las paces que ya ellos sabían muy bien que veníamos cuatro días antes que yo llegara que un muchacho de Bernalillo de su nación se había venido y ese les había dado noticia de que ya los españoles venían a hacerles guerra y que esa era la causa que en la cañada del Río Grande hallara la gente tan prevenida y oculta y que lo mismo era en todo navajo quienes no querían pelear sino ser nuestros amigos.

Y con esto nos retiramos al real el cual estaba muy inmediato al peñol, poniendo el mayor cuidado que se pudo tener, temiendo sus traiciones de estos bárbaros por la experiencia que me asiste de tantos años que he lidiado con ellos por que no lograsen algún descuido.

Hay desde la Laguna de San Joseph a Los Peñoles diez y seis leguas todo por mala tierra de embudos sierras y cañadas muy montuosas, que esto fue ocasión que con la oscuridad de la noche de antes se quedaran perdidos seis caballos y en toda esta distancia no hay agua ninguna por ningún modo.

Habiendo poco rato que habían rendido los soldados de caballada el cuarto de modorra se arrojaron violentamente los enemigos dando grandísimos alaridos y salí del real tan a lindo tiempo yo y la gente de guerra que mayor lugar les dimos a agarrar la caballada con una carga que les dieron la retirada hasta el monte y pie de su peñol y aunque los llamaba con el indio intérprete que bajasen a pelear no quisieron diciéndome que en saliendo el sol pelearíamos, que se estaba juntando la gente para acabarnos, que era mucha la caballada y pocos los españoles, que no habíamos de sacar ni un caballo y fue Dios Nuestro Señor servido que amaneciéramos el día doce sin avería ninguna.

Y al salir el sol como nos lo tenían dicho se arrojó al real un crecido número de emboscada a cuya ocasión salí a recibirlos con la mayor parte de mis españoles y gente amiga, dejando la demás en el real y caballada que tenía a mi vista y con esta prevención dí el Santiago. Y anduvieron también todos los señores soldados y gente amiga que envestieron con tal pujanza que luego trató el enemigo de huir a espaldas vueltas para su peñol, hiriendo muchos los nuestros en su retirada siendo tan estrecha la subida de su peñol que era por una escalera, que esto fue causa de verse apretados ya de nuestras armas y como se estorbaban los unos a los otros para su subida, se extraviaron algunos, los cuales murieron a vista de los suyos que los veían arrastrar y quitarles sus cabelleras.

Hice bastante diligencia por ganarles el peñol y subida para desalojarlos de allí y no pude conseguir más que hasta llegar a la escalera que era adonde ponían la mayor fuerza, jareando y rodando peñascos. Y reconocido lo imposible que era el ganarles dicho peñol y que no se podía sacar de aquí sino que me baldaran la gente como lo iban haciendo, hiriendo dos compañeros y tres indios y que era gastar las municiones sin provecho alguno, traté de retirarme.

Que lo hice con mucha pausa bajándome a mi real dejando [a] los enemigos llorando y con mucha confusión de ver a sus compañeros muertos. Me estuve en este paraje como cosa de dos horas para salir porque no juzgase el enemigo que iba de huída. Y luego salí marchando y fui a plantar mi real distante media legua de estos peñoles, que todo este distrito fui talando milpas. Y fue Dios servido de que este día me llovió un copioso aguacero que hubo suficiente para que bebiese toda la caballada que pasaba el número de más de setecientas bestias con las de los Indios amigos. Y luego que cesó el aguacero y se acabó la tala de las milpas, salí a dormir sin agua cerca de una mesa en donde empezaron a gritar los indios que querían las paces y ser nuestros amigos. Y esta noche hurtaron dos caballos y mataron otro que se les volvió.

El día trece del dicho mes y año salí para un ojo de agua que me dijeron los genízaros había bastante para toda mi caballada y yendo marchando vide[3] unos rastros y luego despaché al capitán de campaña con dos escuadras de señores soldados y cien indios amigos que reconocieran si eran espías de alguna emboscada o iban a alguna ranchería que caso de ser lo uno o lo otro se les hiciese la guerra. Y luego que dí esta orden proseguí mi jornada al dicho ojo de agua y llegado a él fue para mí gran desconsuelo pues no solo no había para la caballada pero así que llegó la gente la consumió. Es tan estéril esta tierra y tan seca que parecía que había diez años que no llovía.

Dejé el real en este dicho puesto y me fui el arroyo abajo más de dos leguas por ver si hallaba alguna agua represada o algunos sartanopales y no topé nada; volví al real y hallé la caballada con la misma necesidad que el día que llegué a Los Peñoles de lo cual me contristé mucho y no desmayé en hacer la diligencia. Volví a salir con la esperanza en Dios y en Su Madre Santísima que me habían de socorrer esta necesidad.

Y habiendo andado al arroyo arriba como una legua topé mi remedio en una cañada ancha de agua y pastos, poblada de muchas milperías todo al propósito de nuestro intento. Volví a mi real muy gustoso dando a todos esta buena nueva donde todos se regocijaron y dieron a Dios las gracias.

Fui a pasar a dicha cañada y aguardar allí al capitán Juan Roque Gutiérrez y gente amiga había ido en su compañía, los cuales llegaron a mi presencia dándome razón de todo lo que les había sucedido y visto que fue el que estando talando milpas se les arrojó el enemigo a despojarlos de allí los cuales dieron tan apretadamente sobre él que luego se puso en huída y los siguieron gran parte de las mesas. Y a los que vinieron a caballo les sucedió lo mismo; se les quitó encima de un peñol como treinta ovejas y carneros que todos vinieron muertos al real; repartióse entre la gente amiga y soldados. También me dieron razón que a la cañada arriba habían bastante sartenopales con agua y muchas milpas en diferentes cañadas. Este día caminé cuatro leguas por cañadas y mala tierra.

El día catorce del dicho mes y año tracé el armarles un engaño a los apaches y para esto avisé cien indios de guerra de todas naciones que en saliendo el real se subiesen ocultos a la mesa y para esto los animé lo bastante y les dí orden de que cuanto toparan lo llevaran a sangre y fuego, advirtiéndoles también de que en dejando parado mi real iría yo a la punta de la mesa con algunos soldados a entretener los enemigos hablando con ellos mientras ellos lograban el poder acercarse y ganarles las espaldas para que unos y otros a un mismo tiempo les diésemos el castigo que tan merecido tenían.

Y luego que dejé parado mi real salí para la dicha mesa con dos escuadras de señores soldados y alguna gente de los indios amigos. Luego que llegué comenzaron a gritar diciendo que ellos no nos querían hacer mal ninguno que querían dar las paces y que para esto hablaríamos despacio. Fuíles manteniendo y dilatando la conversación dando tiempo a que se lograse mi intento y llegó a tanto la plática que se determinaron a bajar dos y que enviase yo dos otros al pie de la mesa el cual fue el uno Naranjo y el otro el gobernador del pueblo de Zía para que se abrazasen los unos con los otros apoyándoles yo todos estos designios hasta que viese lograda mi intención. Dí orden a Naranjo y al dicho gobernador que en levantando los nuestros el alarido arriba se abrazasen cada uno con el suyo y lo mataran que para esto llevaban la prevención de un cuchillo oculto cada uno y tras estos bajaron otros dos y yo despaché otros dos de los míos. El uno fue Juan Griego y otro capitán de la guerra con la misma orden que dí a los demás que habían subido.

Platicaron un gran rato y los nuestros a todo esto sin hacer rumor ninguno llegó a tanto el parlamento que llegaron a bajar al pie de la loma dos de ellos a abrazase y hablar conmigo y duró más de dos horas esta plática y yo siempre entreteniéndolos hasta que comenzó a llover y se despidieron y subieron arriba. La ocasión por que los dejé ir de mis manos fue por la gente que tenía arriba y no sabía de ella y luego al instante que se despidieron de mí habiendo subido el primer banco de la mesa asomaron en la cumbre de ella los nuestros que habían sido ya sentidos de una espía que tenían puesta los dichos enemigos quienes a gran prisa se pusieron en huída y los nuestros dieron en su alcanze los de arriba y abajo soldados e indios y yo con diez señores soldados les fui a coger la huída y bajada para que no escapase ninguno de los enemigos.

Y dos que vinieron a dar por esta parte murieron a nuestras manos y los demás arriba a lanzadas y a balazos pues de más de treinta que eran no escaparon más que cinco sin dos con ferocidad[4] se despeñaron sin otras muchas más muertes que ejecutarían los indios amigos en la distancia que anduvieron por encima de la mesa en mujeres y chusma que así lo tienen de costumbre y por más que los he reñido no escarmientan ni hacen caso, sino que los españoles están presentes.

Acabada esta función me retiré a talar milpas, ínterin bajaba toda la gente y luego que hubo llegado me dieron razón los indios amigos como viniendo caminando por encima de la mesa se vino a incorporar con ellos un apache sin saber qué gente era según los tenía terrorizados el temor de nuestras armas. Cogieronlo y lo amarraron para traerlo a mi presencia.

Y preguntándole que adónde iba les respondió que iba a ver al señor gobernador y viniendo caminando los dichos con este preso llegaron a orillas de un peñasco adonde con gran furia se arrojó al precipicio despeñándose y a no zafar el cable esto el que lo traía amarrado consigo va juntamente con el. Retiréme a mi campo a sosegar y descansar de lo pasado dando a Dios gracias de todo en esta función no hubo más que un herido de mi parte y ese fue un indio.

El día quince del dicho mes y año me mantuve en este dicho paraje de Nuestra Señora de Guadalupe por mi puesto por hallado una estampa suya que les envió con una apache vieja el reverendo padre fray Agustín de Colina a los capitanes de estas partes.

Este día lo gasté en acabar de talar sus milpas enviando escuadras por diferentes cañadas y mesas a recorrer la tierra, las cuales vinieron y me dieron razón que ni uno ni apaches parecían que estaba todo en silencio como si tal gente no hubiera en el mundo y viniendo yo de talar en una cañada muy inmediata a la sierra divisaron los compañeros que venían conmigo un indito y no hallaron más rastro que el suyo adonde descurrió que de temor hasta sus hijos dejan perdidos según estaba de flaco y engerido. Todo esto sucedió en tierras nunca vistas de españoles hasta estos tiempos por mi descubiertas.

Acto de 16 de agosto 1705 años

En este paraje de Nuestra Señora de Guadalupe en diez y seis días del dicho mes y año, yo el dicho maestre de campo cabo y caudillo de la gente de guerra que en dicho paraje se halla haciendo la guerra a sangre y fuego a los enemigos infieles de nación apache habiéndoles hecho el ejemplar castigo que merece su osadía robos y muertes que nos han hecho quebrando las paces que mantuvieron tiempo de diez años el cual consta en estos autos de guerra.

Habiendo reconocido lo hostilizados y temerosos que están pues en el término de tres días que me he mantenido en dicho paraje en varias veces que se ha salido a recorrer la tierra diferentes escuadras por distintos embudos mesas y cañadas tierras adonde en ningunos tiempos han entrado nuestras armas no se puede coger ni hallar ninguno ni aun sus rastros de lo horrorizado que están habiendo puesto su retirada muy lejos de nuestro campo pues aún no son osados ni aun a levantar humos en sus altas tierras.

Tengo por conveniente el llamar a junta de guerra a los oficiales vivos y cabos militares y señores reformados para con parecer de todos resolver lo más conveniente al servicio de ambas majestades y crédito de las armas y desempeño de mi obligación proponiéndoles el si conviene el proseguir más adelante o que se retirasen las armas a su real presidio.

Y yo a dar cuenta de todo a mi gobernador y capitán general quien determinará y dará las providencias más convenientes para en lo de adelante y que si conviene el proseguir la de vuelta al Río Grande no me alivia el trabajo ni rigurosa hambre que padecemos.

A lo que respondieron todos juntos a un mismo fin el que si fuera conveniente el proseguir y reconocieron el que se le podía hacer más daño a el enemigo era bien el proseguir aunque fuera con muchos trabajos y que el enemigo siempre se había de ir ocultando y retirando de donde pudieran ser ofendidos por el temor que han cobrado a nuestras armas en los avances que se les han dado.

Que hallan por imposible el poder hacerles por la presente más [sic] más castigo del que hasta aquí se les ha hecho sin pérdida ninguna de nuestra parte sino en todo prósperos sucesos y que así hallan por conveniente el que se retiren las armas a su real presidio ínterin se descuida el enemigo de la vigilancia con que a la presente está y entonces si en este tiempo no van pecho por tierra a pedir y asentar las paces. Aquí me persuado por cuanto en el puesto del ojo de agua que llamamos de Nuestra Señora nos pusieron cerca de un peñaso 14 cruces señaladas en el suelo y otros caracteres de paz.

Se les puede volver a hacer la guerra con más conveniencias que la presente por estar ya todos capaces en la tierra sus entradas y salidas y se vendrá con más alimentos pues les consta que muchos señores soldados están enfermos de no comer más que elotes y que estos ya no los hay y que como tan servidores de su majestad hallan como católicos el que se retiren las armas que esto lo firmaran para que conste en todo tiempo.

Y reconocido por mi dicho maestre de campo Roque de la Madrid lo acertado y bien fundadas razones de sus pareceres lo hallo por muy conveniente al servicio de ambas majestades y es el mío el de todos retirando las armas de este país hasta otra ocasión firmando estos autos juntamente con mi secretario de guerra.

Juan Roque Gutiérrez [rúbrica] Joseph Domínguez [rúbrica]
Tomás Holguín [rúbrica] Cristóbal de Arellano [rúbrica]
Miguel de Herrera [rúbrica] Martín García [rúbrica]

60 / The Navajos in 1705

Mateo Trujillo [rúbrica] Cristóbal Serna [rúbrica]
José de Naranjo [rúbrica]
Roque Madrid [rúbrica]
Ante mi, Secretario de Guerra
Antonio Castrillón [rúbrica]

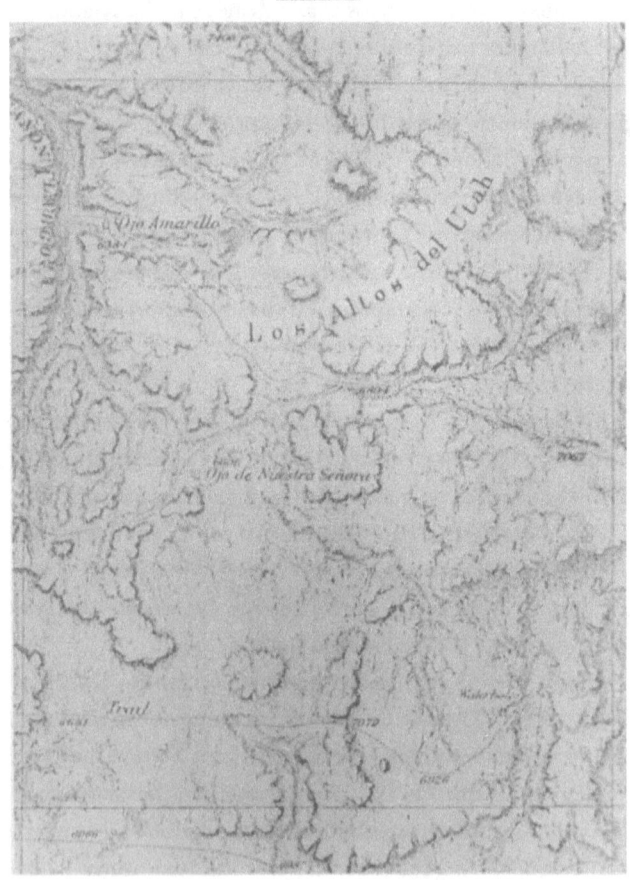

16 / Ojo de Nuestra Señora, on Wheeler Survey atlas sheet no. 69, issued in 1882; actual elevation is 6,550 feet.

El día diez y seis del dicho mes y año salí marchando la devuelta a mi real presidio. Caminé este día al sur acabando de talar las milpas por el camino sin haber rumor de gente humos ni verse rastros de los atemorizados que quedaban del castigo en estos autos referido. Habiendo andado como cosa de seis leguas llegué al ojo de agua de Nuestra Señora adonde senté mi real y dormí esta noche.

El día diez y siete me dieron razón en este dicho paraje de que había milpas y rancherías muy inmediatas a el de la gente que está de paz en los pueblos de la Laguna y Acoma por cuya razón no moví las armas contra ellos por que estén en la inteligencia de que los españoles no le hacen guerra sino a sus enemigos y a los que dicen que no lo son les guardan todo seguro.

Salí este dicho día marchando siempre con la gente al sur; caminé por cañadas y mala tierra hasta llegué a una cañada de muchos sartenjales de agua adonde hice alto y traté de despachar al capitán Juan Roque Gutiérrez a dar breve relación al señor gobernador y capitán general de todo. Caminé este día seis leguas.

Salí de este paraje el día diez y ocho de dicho mes y año. Caminé con el mismo rumbo hasta llegar al ojo del Espíritu Santo. No me sucedió cosa memorable que poner por escrito. Caminé este día siete leguas.

El día diez y nueve del dicho mes y año salí del dicho ojo de agua para el pueblo de Zía adonde me alojé con mi real. Caminé este día siete leguas.

De este dicho pueblo que es el primero de esta cristiandad paso con el real a presencia del señor gobernador y capitán general para que vista esta relación y autos de guerra disponga su señoría lo más conveniente. Y para que conste lo firmé en dicho pueblo con mi secretario de guerra en veinte de agosto de mil setecientos y cinco años.

Roque Madrid [rúbrica]
Ante mi, secretario de guerra,
Antonio Alvarez Castrillón [rúbrica]

The Route

In a campaign of only twenty days, Mre. de campo Roque Madrid led approximately four hundred soldiers, citizen militia, and Pueblo Indian auxiliaries through little-known country in northwestern New Mexico, fought three battles with the Navajos, and suffered only five men wounded and one killed. A later historian stated that between forty and fifty Navajos had been killed.[1] The New Mexico army rode more than 18 miles each day while on the march, over a total distance of about 104 leagues, or 312 miles. Editor Wilson retraced much of this route on the ground between 1971 and 1988.

The lasting testament of this campaign is the journal. It gives the earliest look at the country, as well as some inconsistent comments about what was known before. In the first days after starting off, the war captains of the Tewa and Picuris pueblos, "who knew those mountain ranges and woodlands," made a bleak assessment of what lay ahead. Dismissing their fears, Roque Madrid set off "by a route no Spaniard or person from any other nation had taken until now." On the tenth day, as they approached the Laguna de San Joseph, we learn abruptly of "the map, which was the principal guide of all my company." What this map showed we are not told, but had it survived, it would be as great a historical treasure as the journal itself. Near the end, Madrid claimed that "all this occurred in lands never before seen by Spaniards."

So while soldiers and settlers clearly lacked familiarity with this country, someone (perhaps among the Pueblo allies) knew at least the routes for entering and exiting the Navajo lands, and even had a map.

Very few recognizable place-names were used. Two names that the expedition left have persisted, although west of the Rio Grande scarcely any of their names ever appeared on maps. No other campaigns are known to have followed this same route. How then in the face of these problems (a route seldom used, no surviving map, and few identifiable place-names) could one expect to reconstruct a campaign trail almost three hundred years old? The answer is that it had to be done on the ground and by a process of elimination, using the journal as a guide.

The principal reason for working out the route was to identify the sites of the three battles, only one of which occurred at a named location—Los Peñoles—a name long since forgotten. To retrace the route continuously from beginning to end proved unworkable. Instead it was worked out in segments, primarily by backtracking from Zia Pueblo as far as the vicinity of Chama, New Mexico. It was too much to expect that inscriptions on rocks or other physical evidence might have survived, and none was found.

Numerous maps were consulted, but the most useful ones were Atlas Sheets 69, 69B, and 69D, issued by the U.S. Geographical Surveys West of the 100th Meridian, or the Wheeler Survey, in 1882, 1878, and 1876, respectively. These detailed and relatively accurate maps showed many place-names and routes of travel. The larger-scale 69B and 69D sheets even included odometer distances between settlements. Between them these sheets encompassed all of the country covered by the expedition, to within a few miles of Zia Pueblo.

One important consideration, critical at times, was that the route had to be passable for the army's seven hundred horses. Trails that might have been usable only by smaller parties or people on foot therefore could not be seriously considered.

The journal recorded the length of each day's march in leagues with few exceptions, but it proved impossible to calculate any consistent equivalent between leagues and miles. In general Roque Madrid's leagues were longer than the 4.2 km. or 2.6 miles per league often cited for New Mexico. For example both Diego de Vargas in 1692 and fray Atanasio Domínguez in 1776 gave the length of the route from San Juan to Picuris Pueblo as 8 leagues (Roque Madrid omitted the length of his first day's march). The Wheeler Survey Atlas Sheet 69D represents this distance over the same route as 25.88 miles, or 3.23 miles/league. Farther to the west, the odometer mileage between the third battle site and the Ojo de Nuestra Señora (Otero Ranch Spring) is 16.7 miles. Madrid recorded this distance as 6 leagues, resulting in 2.78 miles/league. Because of such discrepancies, the best indicators of the army's route proved to be the topography, bearings, and occasional place-names. Distances were used only as relative measures.

The muster was held in the plaza of San Juan de los Caballeros Pueblo, located then as now a few miles north of Española, New Mexico. With a late start that first day, 31 July 1705, the troops set out marching northward along the east side of the Rio Grande (their Río del Norte) and made camp after about 3 leagues, probably at the same spot where both Gov. Diego de Vargas and Roque Madrid stayed the evening of 4 October 1692.[2] This would have been at or near modern Velarde, New Mexico.

The next morning they took a cutoff through Embudo Pass, on the eastern side of the broad tableland called La Mesita. At the time, this was the main road. Arriving at Embudo Creek, they followed upstream a short distance and then took the established road to the north side of the stream, nearly identical with present NM route 75, as far as Picuris Pueblo. Father Domínguez described the same route in 1776.[3] That night the army camped 1/4 league or perhaps 3/4 mile west of Picuris.

On 2 August the troops marched west-northwest through rugged hills in the direction of La Cieneguilla, now Pilar, New Mexico, on the Rio Grande. Their trail, which ran between Copper Hill and La Sierrita, lay along the route indicated on Wheeler Survey Atlas Sheet 69 and on modern U.S. Geological Survey and Forest Service maps. In 1854 First Lt. John Davidson and his sixty dragoons would follow this same course to their disastrous defeat by the Jicarilla Apaches, just 3 miles from Cieneguilla.[4] After winding through the hills, the trail exited through Agua Caliente Canyon, which debouches into the Rito Cieneguilla east of Pilar. At some point, Madrid split away from his force to meet with his chaplain and forty Indians from Taos, at the spring called La Cieneguilla. After this all followed the main company and made camp on the bank of the Rio Grande west of present-day Pilar.

On the third morning, the troops ascended the west side of the Rio Grande Gorge at some place above Pilar and then rode northward for 10 leagues to their next campsite, at the Piedra del Carnero. According to Pearce, the Tewa name for Tres Piedras is "mountain sheep rock place," for which Piedra del Carnero would be an acceptable translation.[5] The straight-line distance from Pilar is about 28 miles, and several of the Bernardo de Miera y Pacheco maps of New Mexico from 1777 to 1779 show a Piedra del Carnero at this same location. This campsite at Tres Piedras on the night of 3 August was evidently an established one.

From this point until the afternoon of 9 August, we have not worked out the route on the ground and can only speculate as to where the army went. The coining of a place-name, Sierra Florida, for the complex of mountains and ridges to the west and north of Tres Piedras indicates that they were entering unfamiliar country. At that season, it must have been lush indeed, with good pasturage and a diversity of summer wild flowers. On 4 August the company initially marched west, paralleling what is now highway US 64. They would have reached the Río Tusas and probably followed it upstream, camping on its banks that night.

The following day, 5 August, the troops continued westward for several more leagues, then stopped and rested for a day, while the war captains reconnoitered ahead and then returned to report. On the seventh, the maestre de campo turned north and apparently followed the line of the mountains, passing through spruce forests and eventually coming out into a well-watered valley that he named the Valle de Santiago. By this time they could see ahead of them the Sierra de las Grullas, identified traditionally and also by the Miera maps as the San Juan Mountains, in southern Colorado. By the eighth, Madrid and his men may have reached as far north as the Río de los Pinos, which perhaps was their Río de las Grullas. This flowed from west to east, and it is tempting to think that the place where it split two eminent peaks is Toltec Gorge. In any event the company was now traveling west, not far south of the San Juan Mountains. Today this country is part of the Carson and Rio Grande National Forests. It still has few roads.

The ninth was a long day. The army reached the Chama River quite early, possibly as far north as southern Colorado, and there is no reason to think that their Chama was any other than the present river. They followed it downstream toward the south, past the present site of Chama, New Mexico, until it entered a spacious valley, perhaps near the modern junction of highways NM

17 and US 64-84. Here the troops and auxiliaries paused until the scouts returned once again, whereupon part of the company launched into a spirited argument over their strategy beyond that point. Some of the Pueblos knew where they were and, as usual, were hesitant about going forward.

Two new place-names were introduced here; Los Peñoles, which we come to learn meant Santos Peak and Magdalena Butte, and Río Grande, referring to the present San Juan River.[6] Both lay miles to the west, and no one was quite sure where they were, but they figured in the argument over strategy. This becomes clear by reference to the local geography, and an unwitting result of the debate was the explanation of a seventeenth-century term, *casa fuerte,* associated with the Navajo country.

The basis for the controversy was a long ridge line that still lay a few miles ahead. This ridge extends southeast and then almost due south from present-day Dulce, New Mexico, for more than 25 miles, until it merges with a still higher and more mountainous system west of Llaves, New Mexico. The country just to the west is a series of rugged, low mountains called the Tapicitos on some maps. The eastern side is steep enough to block passage, and the ridge line is broken at only five places, making it an admirable natural defense—a casa fuerte. The only way into the old Navajo country from the east was through one of these five passes, all of them easily watched or guarded. A series of natural lakes (Enbom, Boulder, and Stinking lakes) forms a north-south chain in the long valley that parallels the ridge system on the east.

Dirucaca and Pamuje wanted the army to enter Navajo country in the enemy's rear, by way of the San Juan River. The implication was that the Navajos were known to be living south of the San Juan. However, neither Dirucaca nor anyone else knew how to get to the river, nor was anyone aware of the Navajo River, just ahead, which flows into the San Juan. The proposal by the Jemez genízaros, to head straight for Los Peñoles, would have seen the army pass through the gap at Cisneros Canyon, west of Stinking Lake, and continue almost due west along Compañero Arroyo and Cereza Canyon, south of the huge mesa known as Tuckers Ridge, to enter Navajo lands just south of Los Peñoles.

Two other routes, not part of the argument, would have been via Stock Driveway Canyon, southwest of Stinking Lake, an indirect way that leads to the southwest and would only have served for entering from the south; and through the gap west of Boulder Lake to the headwaters of La Jara Canyon. This canyon runs west for some miles as a broad cañada, until it narrows and becomes impassable west of La Jara Spring. A fourth way would have been to follow the Navajo River from the Dulce area to the San Juan. All of these were followed in Wilson's attempt to retrace the expedition, but the fit of their geography, when compared with the journal, proved to be impossible. When Roque Madrid decided that they would go forward by way of the Rio Grande (that is, the San Juan), perhaps he whispered to himself, 'if we can find it.'

With the matter decided for now, the troops marched away from the valley of the Chama toward the west or southwest. They soon spotted and captured two Indian women, one a Jemez and the other an Apache (Navajo), these two being the first natives or signs of anyone for a week. Interrogation of the prisoners yielded no new information, and the troops continued southward for about 2.5 leagues, to where the scouts caught up again. The maestre de campo then changed the direction of march and rode north, or probably more toward the northwest, through the valleys of Willow Creek and the Cañada de Tío Roques, continuing along present US 64 as far as Briggs Mesa, north of Monero, New Mexico. He assumed this was the summit of the mountain range. The rest

17 / *The campsite of 9–10 August 1705. Looking south along the cañada.*

of his company came up, and they all rode westward as far as a brush-choked cañada. Here, about 2.4 miles east of Dulce and some 2 miles north of US 64, they camped the night of 9 August, on the south-facing slope of the cañada, just below a broad saddle or divide. This area is now open, rather than brushy.

The next morning brought a surprise. Juan Roque Gutiérrez set off to water the horses at the San Juan, but came to the Navajo River (then unnamed) only 1/4 league from the campsite. This river lay at the base of a gentle downslope 0.7 mile north of the saddle in the canyon. This cañada is the first place east of Carracas Mesa where one can reach the Navajo River from the south or east without having to climb down bluffs, ledges, or high banks. It would be the only practical watering place for a horse herd at the Navajo River.

The troops made an early start that day, expecting to find the Navajos at any time. Although the newly found river flowed west, no one realized that by following it they might soon reach the San Juan. Instead they chose the fifth port of entry, the gap in the ridge line just south of Dulce, and headed south up the broad cañada now called Dulce Canyon, parallel with present-day US 64. The company continued to the base of Burns Hill, about 5 leagues from their last campsite and 11 miles south of Dulce. Here they found some tracks and crosses the Navajos had left, and called another war council. No one had spotted them, and Madrid ordered everyone up the steep slope that must indeed have required some effort, especially with a large horse herd. Through a gap at the top, they saw, almost a mile to the south, the shallow lake they were to name the Laguna de San Joseph.

This laguna was a key landmark for identifying the route, and it proved to be a very elusive one. No map of any date or origin showed such a place-name. The journal did not record the distance from the campsite of 9–10 August. From 1971 until 1988, efforts were made to identify any of the present-day lakes south of Dulce with the geography of the lake in the journal, and when this ultimately failed, the same was tried with the Laguna Seca, south of La Jara Mesa. This failed as well, because the only exits lay through an impassable canyon or down steep cliffs. Dulce, John Mills, La Jara, and other lakes in that country are artificial.

In 1988, while speculating that the natural hay meadows alongside US 64 had probably been shallow lakes in prehistoric times,

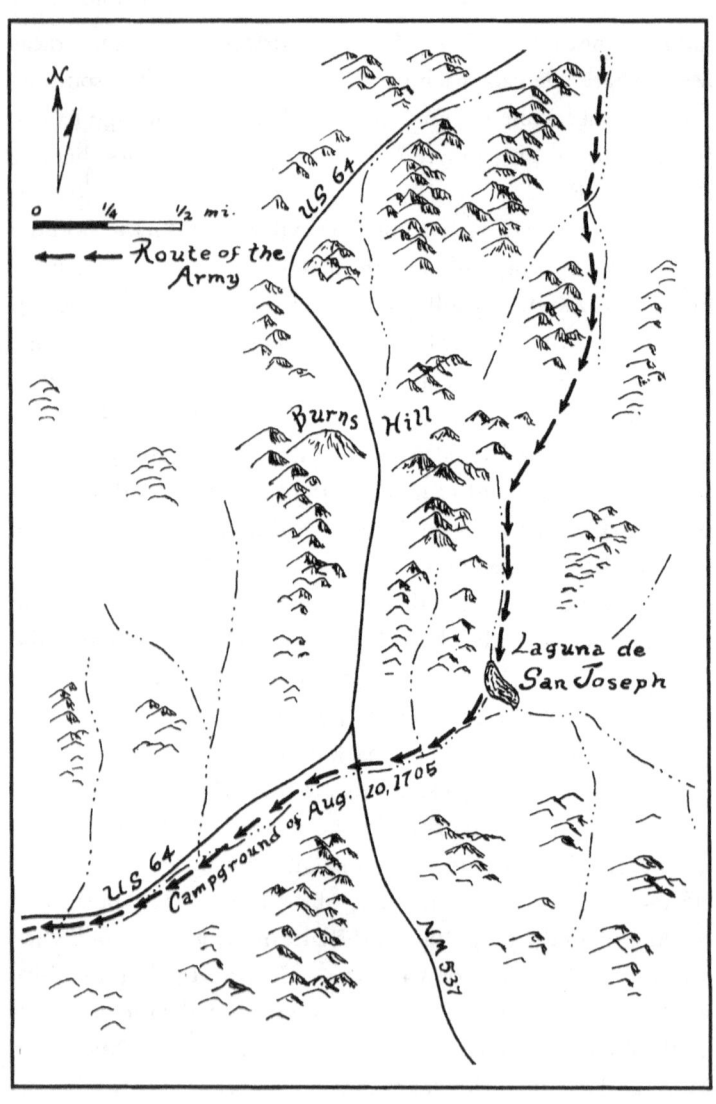

Map 2
The Laguna de San Joseph

the realization dawned that the Laguna de San Joseph must have been a lake that no longer existed. This proved to be the answer. Examination of USGS maps showed that the most likely topographic location beyond Dulce was an embayment between three ridge systems in the upper part of Burns Canyon, about 1/2 mile east of the junction of US 64 and NM 537. The small valley there, where three canyons come together, conformed with the journal description for the Laguna de San Joseph.

The laguna has not entirely disappeared; a vestige of it still exists. On the east side, a strong spring flows from the ground. Its water chemistry reveals it to be highly saline, with dissolved calcium, magnesium, and bicarbonate salts, satisfactory for livestock use.[7] A small marsh with reeds and sedges lies below and adja-

18 / *The Laguna de San Joseph, a shallow marsh as of 1988. View from the northwest.*

cent to it, and by the topography it appears that these waters ponded at one time to form a large pond or shallow lake with a surface area of from 2 to 3 acres. The water now drains away from the marsh through two channels, one along the south or southwest side of the cienega and the other to the northwest side. Between these channels the meadowland is dry and also slightly higher than the laguna area just to the northeast.

The Laguna de San Joseph was formed by spring waters ponding behind a natural dam. At some point in the last 250 years, perhaps during a time of high water, the overflow ran to either side of the dam and began to cut channels, one along the northwest side and the other along the south side of the valley, draining toward the southwest. Sometime in this century, the Bureau of Indian Affairs built a dam in the narrowest part of the valley, about 0.2 mile below the old laguna and trapped the spring waters in a stock pond 1 to 2 acres in extent. Beyond this pond, immediately south and west of the junction of US 64 and NM 537, lies Roque Madrid's spacious meadow with abundant pasturage, where the army rested during the afternoon of 10 August. The actual distance from the campsite the previous night to the Laguna de San Joseph is 16.3 miles, or about 5 1/2 leagues. No other topographic situation was found that satisfied the requirements of the journal.

At five in the afternoon with the sun still high, the company resumed its march westward down Burns Canyon and then along Vaqueros Canyon, generally parallel with modern US 64. They continued for about 14 miles, or between 4 and 5 leagues, halted while a squad went ahead to reconnoiter, then resumed at around three in the morning. The lower part of Vaqueros Canyon constituted what Madrid called the most indomitable land, with rocks, tangled brush, and arroyos. Its appearance is not much different today, although the presence of US 64 makes passage through it much easier.

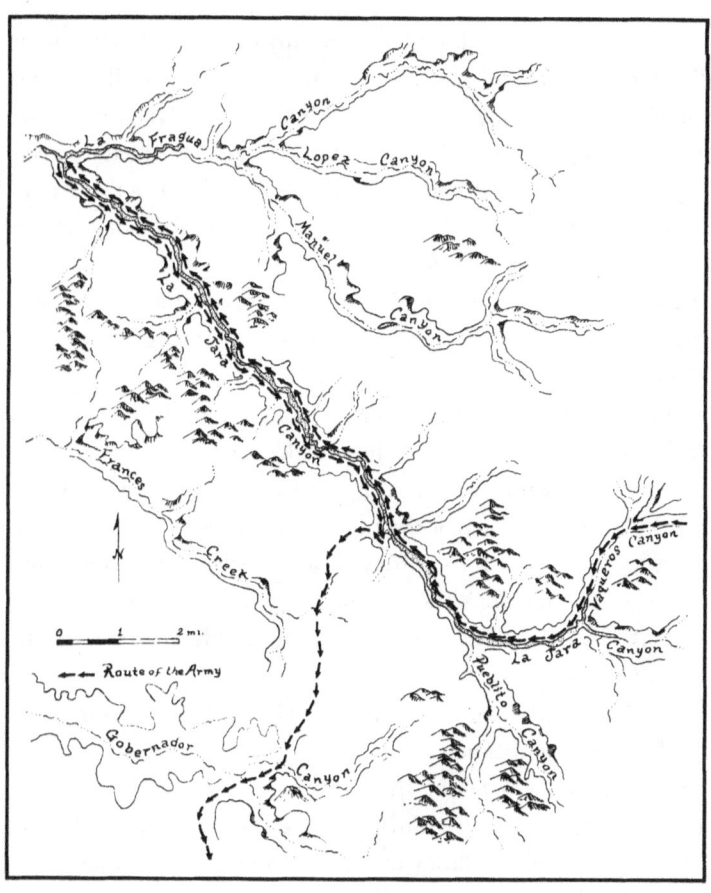

Map 3
The Dawn Assault Through La Jara Canyon

Apart from a three-hour halt the army traveled all night along Vaqueros Canyon, through unfamiliar and potentially hostile country. Upon request, the New Mexico State University Astronomy Department calculated that with an error factor of two days, the moon on the night of 10 August 1705, was a three-day-old crescent that would have been up for most of the day, and in the western hemisphere for about three hours after sunset. The army not only marched at night through virtually unknown country, but for most of the night they had only starlight to see by. They lost six horses in the darkness.

The troops finally came out of the rocks and brush at the mouth of the canyon, where it joins the broad, sandy bottom of La Jara Canyon. Upstream to the east, La Jara Canyon is narrow and confined. The army halted at the first Navajo milpa and changed to fresh horses in preparation for a dawn attack on whomever and whatever lay ahead. Although they had still not found the San Juan River, there was no question that they had arrived at the Navajo settlements.

The mounted squadrons slashed and burned their way through the Navajos' fields and homes along La Jara Canyon for more than 4 leagues, which took them to about the junction of La Jara and La Fragua canyons. This is where the flat, unincised wash wending through La Jara Canyon becomes a narrow rocky canyon. The 4-league stretch would have been well–suited for maize cultivation by planting in the elbows and meanders of the broad, sandy wash. The flat, gently sloping plain that borders the eastern side of the wash might have been just as suitable, because of a series of seep springs at the base of the talus slope there. The natural subsurface irrigation from these springs now supports a very heavy growth of sagebrush, four-wing saltbush, and occasional chamisa.

19 / The mouth of Vaqueros Canyon, staging point for the assault on the Navajos' cornfields in La Jara Canyon, 11 August 1705.

With everything destroyed along this cañada and only two horses injured, the soldiers stopped long enough to eat some of the ears of tender maize and then climb out of La Jara Canyon. The western side of this canyon would have been very difficult terrain indeed, and the best location for getting the horses up was probably where an oil-and-gas road now ascends, about 1.5 miles north of US 64. One-half mile west from the canyon rim there, and standing on a low crest, one can see two prominent peñoles, or peaks—Santos Peak and Magdalena Butte—in plain view to the south-southwest, about 9 miles distant in a straight line. From

20 / *Santos Peak and the canyon country beyond,
from the western end of Magdalena Butte, summer 1972.*

any farther west however, a mesa south of the highway blocks the two peaks from sight. The army advanced toward Los Peñoles, pillaging and burning.

At one time or another, editor Wilson climbed all of the isolated peaks in the old Navajo country east of Cañon Largo and typically found little or nothing by way of cultural remains. The exception was Santos Peak, a high narrow pinnacle that becomes more impressive as one approaches it. It rises about 500 feet above the valley floor to the north, and the uppermost parts are sheer, except for one place on the north side where a hazardous ascent can be made to the flattened top. The top is about 3/4 acre in extent and contains at least eight stone rings, the remnants of early

21 / On top of Santos Peak, with rocks still piled along the northern edge for hurling down on enemies below, summer 1971.

Navajo hogans, in addition to Navajo and Pueblo pottery. Along the north edge above the place of ascent, there are still piles of rocks waiting to be hurled down at any besiegers. This site was recorded as LA 8948.

A collection of pottery from LA 8948 included Navajo utility and painted types, in addition to a dozen puebloan sherds. Ms. A. H. Warren of the Museum of New Mexico examined them and concluded that the ceramics dated between A.D. 1650 and 1750, perhaps from the last part of the seventeenth century.[8] A piñon sample collected there yielded a tree-ring date of 1364P–1695vv, with the latter probably quite close to the death date for the tree.[9] Nothing indicated a subsequent reoccupation.

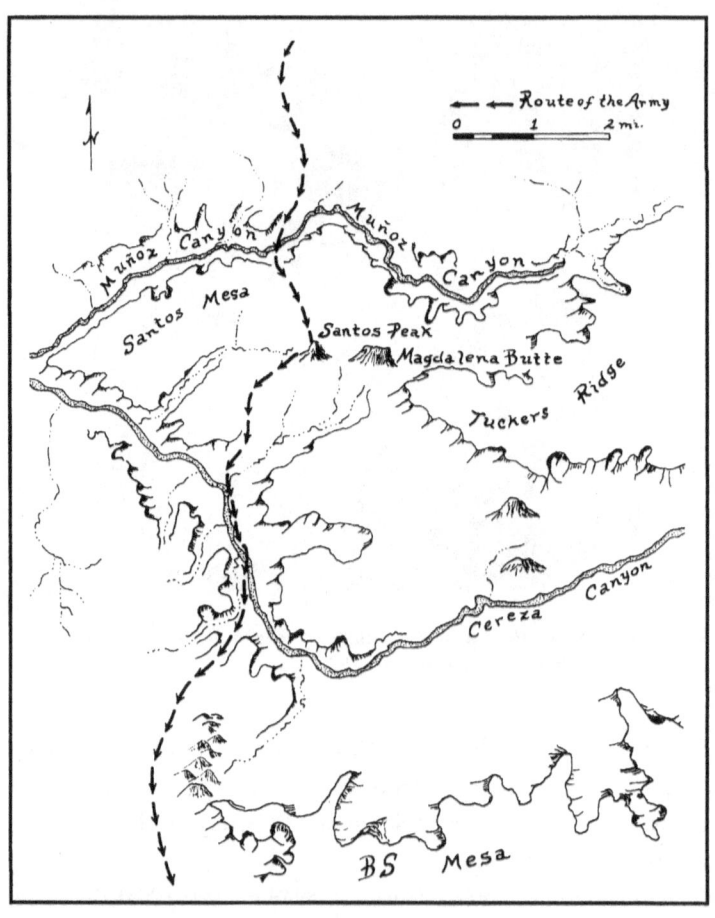

Map 4
Los Peñoles: Santos Peak and Magdalena Butte

Magdalena Butte, 1/2 mile to the east, is slightly higher than Santos Peak and up to 1/4 mile in length across the top. Most of its sides are sheer near the top, although ascent is easy from the east side. The top is covered with rolling sand dunes and bears no signs of Navajo occupation, the pottery there being almost all prehistoric in age. Santos Peak and Magdalena Butte are the only two peñoles that are close together and visible from near the west side of La Jara Canyon.

One objection to this identification of Santos Peak and Magdalena Butte might be that the journal says it was 16 leagues from the Laguna de San Joseph to Los Peñoles. By odometer the distance is 32.7 miles, or about 11 leagues. The calculated distance from the campsite on the night of 9–10 August to the laguna, however, is some 16.3 miles, or 5 1/2 leagues, which would give 16 1/2 leagues from that camp to Los Peñoles. The scribe probably erred and wrote the overall figure for the distance marched on 10 and 11 August, even though he indicated that it was from the laguna to Los Peñoles. Comments made later imply that forays to the side were not counted as part of a day's march.

The battle at Santos Peak on 12 August was fought with courage and determination on both sides, the Navajos losing an unknown number killed and wounded, while the New Mexicans lost five wounded. Madrid's forces did amazingly well to fight their way to the base of the ladder at the place of ascent, which is at the top of a steep talus slope that offers no protection, just 25 feet below the top of the peñol. The Navajos' position could not be taken, and the battle resulted in a tactical victory for them.

For the balance of the campaign, the journal says very little about the direction(s) of the march, and indeed the troops spent much time destroying milpas. In general they rode southward. At the conclusion of fighting on 12 August, Madrid apparently withdrew a short distance and rested for two hours, then set off and moved 1/2 league until a downpour caught them and the troops halted again. After the rain let up, the company started off once more and halted for the night near a mesa. The only mesas in the area are Santos Mesa, the more elevated parts of which lie about 1/2 league west of the peak, and the isolated northern tip of Albert Mesa, about 1 1/2 leagues to the south. The milpas that they were destroying most likely lay along Cereza Canyon, another broad, shallow wash system.

South of Cereza Canyon lies a broad plateau that the maps call Ensenada Mesa. For 8 or 9 miles, to Cañon Largo on the west and to Tapicito Creek or Canyon on the south, the terrain forms a low, rolling surface without sharp breaks in elevation, the broad ridges separated by mostly unnamed drainage ways. The only useful landmark is Albert Mesa, which is on the north and east side. Natural-gas wells and gas-field roads are found all through this country, but even so it can be confusing for persons unfamiliar with the roads to find their way across Ensenada Mesa. More significantly for Madrid and his men, anyone entering from the north, particularly with a large horse herd, will find their way off the mesa blocked by the lines of bluffs and the short, narrow canyons on the north side of Tapicito Creek and the eastern side of Cañon Largo. One way out would be to follow Cereza Canyon downstream to the west-northwest and eventually reach Cañon Largo that way, but from subsequent journal entries it is clear that the army continued south across Ensenada Mesa on 13 August.

Ensenada Mesa had missed the recent rains, this being the land that was so sterile and dry it seemed that it had not rained in ten years. The only place where the expedition could have found its way off this mesa was identified in 1988, and this agreed with the distances and topography noted in the journal, even with an ab-

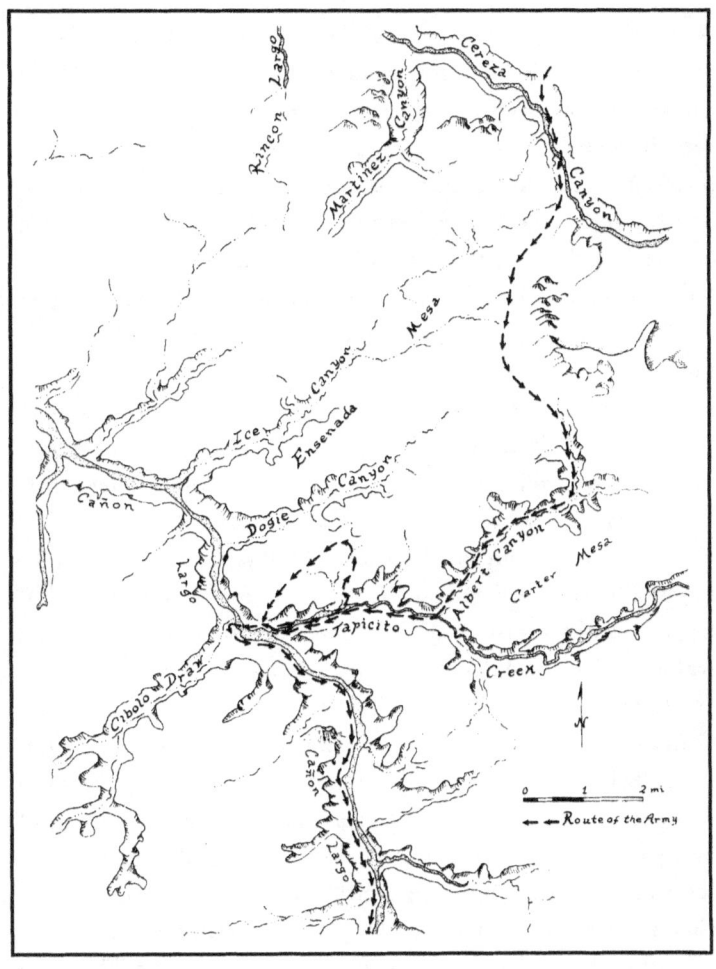

Map 5
The Encounter at the Bluff, Junction of Tapicito Creek and Cañon Largo

sence of bearings. From their camp near Albert Mesa, the men marched south and east for about 4 miles, to the head of Albert Canyon. The floor of this canyon is an uninterrupted natural roadway that extends 3.5 or 4 miles toward the southwest, to its juncture with Tapicito Creek. This creek is another broad cañada, and the company then followed it west to its debouchment in Cañon Largo. Tapicito Creek was presumably the wide cañada with water and pastureland, filled with many milpas. Four leagues would be about right for their march that day, to a camp near the mouth of Tapicito Creek.

Here another confrontation took form on the morning of 14 August. The Navajos had been following the army and now shouted down from the tip of the mesa or bluff above, asking to parley and saying they wanted peace. The only place where this could have happened would have been at the bluff on the north side of the Largo-Tapicito junction, opposite the Truby Ranch, where the bluff forms a nearly sheer face approximately 100 feet in height. Madrid was determined that a fight there not become another standoff.

He evidently sent the presidial troops and militia south up Cañon Largo, as if they were leaving, while he directed a hundred Pueblo warriors to find a roundabout way to the mesa top without letting themselves be seen. Since this "mesa" is a line of bluffs rather than an isolated elevation, the Pueblos had only to return in the direction whence they had come, or continue down Cañon Largo until they found a place to climb the side. In the meantime, Madrid and others kept the Navajos talking. This went on for more than two hours, until the Pueblos arrived in position on top. The Navajos were then caught between the two forces. This time the battle ended with the New Mexicans the victors.

The journal descriptions preceding and during the battle, when viewed against the topography and the stated location 6 leagues

22 / *Pueblito ruin at LA 2298, atop the bluff at the junction of Tapicito Creek and Cañon Largo. The southeast and southwest sides face the camera, autumn 1972.*

north of the Ojo de Nuestra Señora, one of the most securely identified places on the route, combine to leave no doubt that this third encounter was fought on the bluff at the Largo-Tapicito confluence. On top of this bluff and about 20 meters back from the edge, however, stands one of the best-known sites in the old Navajo country, the seven-room pueblito now being called Tapicito Ruin, LA 2298. This site was recorded originally in 1941, rerecorded in 1972, and has become the subject of a considerable literature.[10] If this interesting structure was built in 1694, as the tree-ring dates seem to show, why was it not mentioned in the 1705 campaign journal?

Why indeed? Although the Pueblo auxiliaries were the only ones on top, they could hardly have missed seeing such a structure and undoubtedly would have told the Spaniards about it, leading to an inspection. The absence of any mention of it in the journal strongly suggests that it was not there. A logical conclusion is that the pueblito at LA 2298 had not yet been constructed in 1705, and that whenever it was built, the wood in it was salvaged and reused from another dwelling. The intact roof over one room also argues that the structure is more recent in age. At present there is no way of knowing whether its builders set to work immediately following the August 1705 campaign or at some later time.

The day after the third battle, 15 August, the camp remained at the same location, while Madrid sent his squadrons along the cañadas once more to lay waste more of the milpas. The Navajos, except for one small boy, had disappeared.

On the sixteenth, the maestre de campo called another war council. The consensus was that the men had done as much as they could and it was time to return home, particularly given the fact that they were out of food. The proceedings were formalized for the governor, and everyone set off once again, this time marching south up Cañon Largo to the Otero Ranch Spring, called by them the Ojo de Nuestra Señora. This is the only large spring in a wide area, and when three friars passed that way in 1745, they noted that it was 1 league from the first Navajo settlement.[11] It was still identified as the Ojo de Nuestra Señora on the Wheeler Survey Atlas Sheet No. 69. By odometer it is 16.7 miles south of the location of the last battle.

The large rock mentioned in the campaign journal is still there, although the fourteen crosses have long since vanished. In July 1875, U.S. Army Lt. C. C. Morrison led his survey party past the Ojo de Nuestra Señora and described it as

a fine bubbling spring, situated in a drain running into
Cañon Largo. The ground round about is marshy; large
bowlders [sic] are scattered over the ground, low mesas of
sandstone inclose the drain, and numerous trails concentrate
at this one volcanic spring in the desert.[12]

At the time Wilson visited it in 1972, an informant gave the modern name, Otero Ranch Spring. At that time, too, the spring issued around the rock, actually a sandstone boulder that lies about 70 meters north-northwest from the abandoned ranch house. Since then a large holding tank has been excavated about 100 meters downslope from the rock, at the edge of the valley floor. As of 1988 this tank was well filled, while for about 8 meters below the boulder, the ground was still damp, with a good growth of grasses and sedges. The exposed bedrock around the old ranch bore no inscriptions.

For the next two days, 17 and 18 August 1705, the march was almost leisurely as the company covered 6 and 7 leagues respectively, bearing southeast rather than to the south. The straight-line distance from the Ojo de Nuestra Señora to the Ojo de Espíritu Santo, still known as Holy Ghost Spring, is 50 miles. The Cuba, New Mexico, area, which should already have been known as Nacimiento, was not mentioned. Perhaps they passed to the southwest of the Cuba area; the journal itself gives few details of the route. On their last day in the field, the troops covered another 7 leagues and finally arrived at their destination, Zia Pueblo. There on 20 August 1705, Roque Madrid mustered his men for the last time, in the presence of the governor, and signed the campaign documents. The second expedition to the Navajo country that year was over.

Conclusion

The most immediate result of Roque Madrid's August campaign was another expedition to Navajo country the following month. Little is known of this second punitive campaign, but the two are always mentioned together in most subsequent reports concerning Spanish-Navajo relations under Cuervo y Valdés.

Planning for the September campaign was well under way by the ninth of the month. On that date, fray Juan de Tagle sent a letter-patent to the New Mexico missions, advising them that the governor was preparing a campaign against the Navajos for 26 September.[1] The troops must have left before that date, however, since they had returned to Santa Fe by the first week of October.

The certification of service of José Trujillo, a resident of Santa Cruz de la Cañada and a participant on the September campaign to Navajo country, stated that the troops returned to Santa Fe on 3 October 1705, after having inflicted death on the enemy, taken women and children prisoners, and burned their fields.[2]

Antonio Tafoya recorded his recollection of events many years later, in 1745. According to his testimony, a force of citizens, soldiers, and Indians "to the number of 400" entered Navajo territory by way of the Sierra de las Grullas, some 30 leagues northwest of Santa Fe. They traveled about 18 leagues through a land of many mesas and cañadas, until they found a fair-sized river and some springs and lakes. Tafoya noted that the Navajos planted maize, beans, squash, and watermelon in the cañadas. The land seemed to him dry and sterile. The Spaniards found some ranchos atop the mesas, where they also saw around five hundred Indians, adults and children. The Christian Indian allies killed one of them, which caused the Navajos to flee through the mountains. For that reason, the troops departed for Santa Fe by way of the campsite called the Cerro de los Pedernales, near Abiquiu.[3]

It is difficult to reconcile Tafoya's description and that contained in Roque Madrid's campaign diary with the accounts of the two expeditions that emerged soon after their conclusion. If the later reports are to be believed, the "exemplary punishment" referred to in the diary only hinted at the violence of the August campaign. Tafoya's observation that the Navajos fled after a single Indian was killed, at which time the Spaniards returned home, is completely at odds with the facts as later presented, which are more in line with Trujillo's certification.

Writing in October 1705 to certify Cuervo y Valdés's civil and military service as interim governor of New Mexico, the Santa Fe cabildo stated that they considered the August and September campaigns the second and third successful strikes against the Navajos. Obviously the cabildo was counting the twenty-five-man sortie just weeks after Cuervo y Valdés's arrival in Santa Fe as the first campaign. They further stated that the punishment inflicted on the Navajos on the second and third campaigns was so great with respect to deaths, captive women and children, destruction of milpas, burning of maize and houses, and the plunder of horses and small livestock, along with buckskins, baskets,[4] and other goods, that the Navajos were stunned and filled with fear.[5]

Among the women and children prisoners were many apostates from the Jemez and Tano nations. They had gone to live among the Navajos after the uprisings of 1680, 1694, and 1696.

Some had gone voluntarily and others were captives. They were returned to their pueblos, to the reverend fathers. The cabildo also reckoned that under Cuervo y Valdés's administration up until that time, more than three hundred apostates were restored from Hopi and others from K'iakima.

Fray Juan de Tagle, the Franciscan vice-custos, echoed the remarks of the Santa Fe cabildo. Tagle stated that Cuervo y Valdés had introduced Catholic weapons as far as the center of the Navajos' very remote mountain ranges and impregnable peñoles. The August campaign had horrified the Navajos with so many deaths, captives taken, and the destruction of their milpas. In September they were again horrified by the burning of a large amount of their maize; not even the huts they lived in were spared. Many Navajos were killed, and their women and children captured.[6] Another Franciscan, Father Vélez de Escalante, who conducted research in the Santa Fe archives from 1776 to 1779, echoed Father Tagle's observations, adding that forty to fifty Navajos perished as a result of Roque Madrid's expedition.[7]

The booty on both occasions consisted of buckskins, baskets, hides, and some horses and small livestock. A number of people who were living in apostasy as captives since the general rebellion of 1680 and the new revolt of 1696 were returned to the missions where they belonged. What is more, the Spaniards went into Navajo country by different routes in August and September. This had been tried unsuccessfully in the past, and the impenetrable nature of their lands had led the Navajos to grow bold.

Cuervo y Valdés's own comments further attest to the true nature of the Navajo campaigns. Writing to the viceroy of New Spain, the Duque de Alburquerque, on 23 October 1705, he remarked that during the bloodiest of wars punishing the enemy Navajos, he learned that the province of Zuni was experiencing serious unrest and sent a squadron there too. Before the next month was out, Cuervo y Valdés wrote to the king to tell him that that year alone he had returned more than four hundred Christians, some captives and other apostates, to their respective pueblos and missions. Presumably this included people from Zuni and Hopi, as well as those from Navajo country. Taking into account the figure of over three hundred cited by the cabildo of Santa Fe as having come from Hopi and Zuni, it would follow that no more than one hundred Pueblos had been brought back from Navajo country as a result the August and September campaigns.[8]

The matter of Pueblo Indian refugees among the Navajos is one of many implications that will have to be worked out anew. In discussing the documentary evidence for such refugees remaining in the Dinetah country after 1696, Hogan stated that Roque Madrid's campaign journal and Reeve's summary of it provided the only statements directly supporting such a conclusion.[9] Actually this is not the case; the single Pueblo Indian whom Roque Madrid found among the Navajos was the Jemez woman, apparently married to a Navajo and living there voluntarily. She was one of the two whom he put to torture on 9 August. A number of documents that may not have been available to Hogan clearly state that "many" Pueblo Indians who had been living among the Navajos, some since as early as 1680, were returned to their respective missions and pueblos following the Navajo campaigns of 1705. Specific reference was made also to Jemez and Tano refugees. Unfortunately no actual number is ever mentioned, although the evidence suggests that, as noted above, it did not exceed one hundred people. Blas Martín estimated in 1745 that, when he was in Navajo country at some point during the period 1712 to 1715, more than two hundred Christian Indians were living among the Navajos.[10] All this tends to support Hogan's assertion that no large

CONCLUSION / 93

number of Pueblo Indians was incorporated into the Navajo population. Nevertheless the documents refer only to refugees who returned and not to those who might have remained with the Navajos.

Madrid's campaign journal strongly supports the assertion that the Navajos were principally farmers, not pastoralists. His forces did find evidence of foraging and hunting, and buckskin was a major trade item to the Spaniards. Still the invading force spent most of its time from the eleventh through the fifteenth laying waste to the milpas when not actually fighting. While livestock must have been kept at some distance from unfenced milpas and might have gone unnoticed, the soldiers found only two sheep at Los Peñoles and later killed a herd of thirty sheep and rams; no other livestock was mentioned among the Navajos.

The nature of Navajo agriculture was made quite clear by the examinations of La Jara Canyon and other cañadas as far as Cañon Largo during the retracement of the route. Their farms were at the bends or meanders in the broad, sandy washes, where they could expect to raise good crops without irrigating, provided that excessive runoff from summer storms did not wash away the fields. Capt. Juan Mateo Manje described the Gila River Pimas doing exactly the same thing when he passed that way in the spring of 1699.[11] This same system would probably work today along portions of La Jara, Largo, Cereza, Muñoz, and neighboring canyons.

The absence of pueblitos or synonymous terms in the journal comes as no surprise, in view of the testimony years later that these little stone houses were built in response to raids by the Utes and Comanches. Yet the apparent absence of the LA 2298 structure must be explained with regard to the cutting dates of A.D. 1694 for timbers in its construction. Our conclusion is that in 1705 it was not there. The questions of who built it, when, and why, must be a task for subsequent studies.

Another study will have to reconcile Governor Cuervo y Valdes's description of the Navajo country, summarized below, with the limits for the eastern part of that country implicit in Roque Madrid's journal. He found no signs of occupation east of La Jara Canyon, and he left the Navajo milpas behind somewhere during the march from Tapicito Creek south to the Ojo de Nuestra Señora. This is a much more restricted homeland than what Governor Cuervo y Valdés indicated. Cuervo y Valdés of course would have seen all of the campaign journals, though he himself did not go along on the expeditions. Given that Navajo women were found gathering quelites and their men reported hunting well east of La Jara Canyon, it would seem that the governor was indicating that the known limits to Navajo country were not circumscribed by the extent of settlements and milpas.

Particularly interesting is the report of Laguna and Acoma milpas near the Ojo de Nuestra Señora, which would place them well within what we have heretofore thought was Navajo country. The ethnicity of "people at peace in the pueblos of Laguna and Acoma" is not identified in the journal. The term *Jemez genízaros,* used more than once, also needs further explanation.

After the successful conclusion of the second campaign, the Navajos were no longer perceived as a threat to the colony. Early in January 1706, acting as secretary of government and war, alcalde ordinario of Santa Fe, and protector of the Indians of New Mexico, Alfonso Rael de Aguilar certified Cuervo y Valdés's actions as governor. He stated that governors and caciques of the Zuni, Keres, Tewa, Jemez, Tano, Pecos, Tiwa, Picuris, and Taos nations had come before him in Santa Fe to voice their support for the governor for delivering them from the Navajo threat. Soon after his arrival, he had sent men in pursuit of two large groups of Navajos who had taken livestock from San Ildefonso, Santa Clara, and

San Juan. Afterward he had carried out other campaigns against the Navajos, taking along the most experienced Indians. The Pueblo allies had scored victories and avenged themselves; they were also well satisfied with the booty and resulting calm.[12]

In February the Santa Fe cabildo reported that after the final campaign to the Navajo country, most of their captains had come to sue for peace in the name of all the rest. They brought buckskins, baskets, and other things from their country to ransom their women and children, who were living in several Spanish settlements. The governor warmly received the emissaries, giving them many varas of woolen cloth and baize, knives, hands of tobacco, ribbon, beads, and other things they liked. He presented them with hides that they did not have in their country, for which reason they valued them highly. They used buffalo hides for robes and elk hides to make footwear. Many people taken prisoner during the frequent encounters and imprisoned in Santa Fe before Cuervo y Valdés arrived were returned. The captains had come every month since, carrying large, very white buckskins, on which the holy cross was painted and below it the heads of their captains, with the head of the principal captain in the middle. His name as the Spaniards recorded it was Perlaja.[13]

Cuervo y Valdés provided corroborating testimony for the cabildo's report in two letters to the viceroy of April and June, although they differ in some of the details and interpretations of events. The way Cuervo y Valdés understood matters, the captains of the Navajo rancherias had come to Santa Fe to sue for peace on behalf of their principal *caudillo* and *capitán mayor,* Perlaja, who the Navajos considered their "rey y señor." The several private delegations of different captains sought peace; speaking for Perlaja and all the other Navajos, they stated that they were resolved to congregate in settlements and live "como gente," as they themselves put it, and receive the water of holy baptism. For this reason he had made a special gift of the items listed by the cabildo (to which he added hats) to Perlaja.[14]

Cuervo y Valdés shared with the Duque de Alburquerque something of what he had learned about the history, geography, and agricultural practices of the Navajos in the year he had just spent in New Mexico. He stated that the Navajos had waged continuous warfare from the time of the conquest of New Mexico until the 1680 revolt. Then they had continued their assaults from 1693 until 1705, at which time bloody battles won a peace. He described the Navajo country as consisting of separate rancherías stretching from south to north for around 100 leagues, as far as the land of the Utes, Carlanas, and Comanches, and on the east, the Spanish frontier. Forming a semicircular boundary were El Peñasco de las Grullas, the Río San Antonio, the Río de las Jaras, the Río de la Culebra, the old pueblo of Chama, the embudo of the Piedra Lumbre, San Juan Pueblo, Santa Clara Pueblo, San Ildefonso Pueblo, Cochiti Pueblo, San Felipe Pueblo, Santa Ana Pueblo, Zia Pueblo the valley of La Cañada, Chimayo, Picuris, Taos, Bernalillo, Alburquerque, Jemez, the Rio Puerco, Cebolleta, Laguna Pueblo, Acoma, the paraje de Santa Ana, Nacimiento, El Morro, and distant Zuni and Hopi. From the two most distant points, it measured 300 leagues. On a straight line to the west, the Río Grande (San Juan) divided the Dinetah on its way to the sea. On their land they grew maize, beans, squash, chile, and other crops they had found in the Christian pueblos. They wove both wool from their sheep and cotton that they grew.[15]

The military defeat of the Navajos and the subsequent peace had a powerful demonstration effect on the Faraón Apaches. While peace negotiations were being concluded in Santa Fe with the Navajo captains in early 1706, Faraón representatives went to

Pecos Pueblo and met with the alcalde mayor, Juan de Ulibarrí. As had the Navajos, the Faraones presented him with a hide painting. This one depicted a Spaniard and an Apache holding the holy cross as a sign of peace.[16]

To all appearances, Cuervo y Valdés's tactics for dealing with the Navajos had proved successful. The reigning calm in New Mexico gave him the opportunity to take additional action to bolster his entreaties for a regular appointment as governor instead of his interim one. Early in 1706, he founded the villa of Alburquerque in honor of the viceroy of New Spain, Francisco Fernández de la Cueva Enríquez, Duque de Alburquerque. Although he stipulated that he had had the requisite thirty-five families on hand for a legal founding, subsequent investigation revealed that only nineteen families had been present. That same year he resettled eighteen Tano Indians from Tesuque in the abandoned pueblo of Galisteo, a number of Picuris that Juan de Ulibarrí had brought back from El Cuartelejo, and twenty-six Tewa families at Pojoaque. Finally Cuervo y Valdés purported to have resettled twenty-nine families from Santa Cruz de la Cañada, who had spread throughout the valley since its founding, in a new town called Santa María de Grado. The truth of the situation was revealed as soon as he was out of office; the community reverted to its original name.[17]

Years after the events, Cuervo y Valdés embellished his service in New Mexico, still seeking preferment from the crown and bitter that he had not been given the governorship of New Mexico he felt he so richly deserved. He spoke of four successful campaigns fought hand-to-hand against the Navajos. He reported that peace had been made and innumerable apostates had been returned to their missionaries in their *doctrinas* and missions. He recalled that Juan de Ulibarrí's expedition to El Cuartelejo to free the Picuris people had revealed that place to have a million inhabitants. Yet this was nothing more than the hyperbole expected from an unofficial service record. On one point Cuervo y Valdés was completely accurate. When he handed over the government to his successor, the Marqués de la Peñuela, which took place in August 1707, the hard-won peace was still holding.[18]

The coming together of a number of factors led the Navajos to break the peace, apparently by the end of the following year. The newly arrived governor had noted that a drought had resulted in the loss of most of the harvest. Evidence also suggests that a revolt by people from Laguna and Zuni, at the instigation of the Hopis, was narrowly averted. Perhaps the most important element, however, was the character of the new governor himself. The Marqués de la Peñuela openly mocked Cuervo y Valdés's practice of giving gifts to the Indians, even though he continued the policy on at least three occasions. Indian leaders from several pueblos complained that he lacked his predecessor's generosity and failed to halt abuses against them. The governor clearly preferred a military solution for the quickening pace of Navajo raiding.[19]

On 21 February 1709, the Marqués de la Peñuela ordered Roque Madrid to summon ten militiamen from his jurisdiction to go in pursuit of some Navajos who had carried off cows and horses from the vicinity of Santa Clara. José Trujillo and José Naranjo had gone after them and were probably at great risk. Madrid was to borrow horses from the Indians of San Ildefonso, San Juan, and Santa Clara, since the presidial soldiers were in the field and no other mounts were available. He could take along some Indian allies if he deemed it necessary.[20]

A Navajo attack on Jemez on 8 June damaged the church, desecrated the altar, and resulted in the deaths of one Spaniard and several Christian Indians. A Spanish force pursued the Navajos, reportedly killing some twenty.[21]

That winter the governor once again ordered Madrid to lead a force against the Navajos, stating that he had already sent five campaigns to Navajo country in 1709.[22] José Trujillo, who had served on the September 1705 campaign, fought on three of them; he went back to Navajo country in April, June, and September 1709.[23] Still the Navajos continued to invade, kill, and rob. They had sued for peace after the fifth campaign, but then the same people had stolen livestock and killed some Indian herders who were working for citizens of Santa Cruz and others from San Juan Pueblo. Madrid was ordered to punish the Navajos by fire and sword in their mountains, departing on 10 December from San Juan with militiamen and Indian allies. The Marqués de la Peñuela also had a special, unusual command for Madrid. He was not to permit the ceremonial scalp dances that the Pueblo warriors usually performed; he was even ordered to stop them from taking scalps in the event they killed some Navajos.[24]

The nearly constant campaigning of 1709 eventually led to an absence of hostilities lasting four years. It then became clear, however, that the Navajo-Spanish wars were merely in abeyance and had not been concluded. In October 1713, Gov. Ignacio Flores Mogollón ordered Capt. Cristóbal de la Serna, a veteran of the August 1705 campaign, to lead 50 presidial soldiers, 22 militiamen, and 150 Indian allies against the Navajos.[25]

A year later, Roque Madrid took 50 soldiers, some militiamen, and 212 Pueblo Indians to punish the Navajos who had killed an Indian leader from Jemez. Madrid headed up the Chama Valley, going by way of the Piedra Lumbre. He attacked them on several peñoles and in torreones, capturing 7 Navajos and killing around 30. He took from them 200 fanegas of maize, much other grain, and 110 head of small livestock.[26]

Governor Flores Mogollón called upon Captain de la Serna again in October 1716 to lead 40 soldiers, some militiamen, and a troop of Indian allies to Navajo country. The total force of some 400 engaged the Navajos, killing 6 and carrying off around 200 head of small livestock. This was the last major Spanish expedition against the Navajos for the next half century, until the peace was broken in the early 1770s.[27]

From 1678 until 1705, twenty-seven years had elapsed between Spanish incursions into Navajo country. Beginning with Roque Madrid's 1705 campaign and for more than a decade thereafter, full-scale Spanish military expeditions were carried out against the Navajos almost without surcease. One searches in vain for a single answer to explain why the violence suddenly stopped. Utes and Comanches may have come to seem more fearsome foes than the Spaniards in the eyes of the Navajos. The Navajo expansion ever closer to territory occupied by New Mexican colonists may finally have proved counterproductive. Spaniards may have considered crowding near Navajo territory no longer worth the risk. Surely considerable loss of life and property to a superior military force had worn down the Navajos' resistance. In the final analysis, both Navajo and Spaniard must have welcomed a respite from their sanguinary relationship in the opening years of the eighteenth century.

Biographical Sketches

Antonio Alvarez Castrillón

Antonio Alvarez Castrillón was born in 1680.[1] Before coming to New Mexico, he lived in San Sebastián and at the presidio of Pasage in New Biscay. Given that there was a presidio at San Sebastián in Sinaloa until 1686 and that one was subsequently established at Pasage, near Cuencamé, it seems likely that Alvarez Castrillón's father was also a presidial soldier.[2]

In 1705 Antonio was serving with the presidio of Santa Fe. Acting in the capacity of secretary of war to Roque Madrid, he recorded the Navajo campaign of that year in his elegant, flowing hand. That same year, Alvarez Castrillón settled in Santa Fe.

Little more is known of him. By April 1707, he was an alferez with the Santa Fe presidio.[3] In 1710 he held that rank, but was on reserve status.[4] Alvarez Castrillón purchased land and a house in Santa Fe and was still active in presidial affairs in 1714, when he participated in a junta of war that Gov. Ignacio Flores Mogollón convoked.[5]

There is no indication that Antonio Alvarez Castrillón ever married. He was still living in Santa Fe as late as March 1715.[6] Two years later, a relative, Capt. José González Castrillón, died at his Hacienda de San Felipe y Santiago in the jurisdiction of the Real de Nieves, naming Antonio as one of his executors. Alvarez Castrillón was residing at the hacienda in the summer of 1718.[7]

CRISTÓBAL DE ARELLANO

Baptized on 3 May 1665 in Aguascalientes,[8] New Spain, Cristóbal de Arellano was the son of Nicolás de Arellano and Leonor Fernández de Valus Bercerra, who was from Teocaltiche, Jalisco.[9] Prenuptial investigations for Cristóbal's marriage to Graciana Romero were conducted in Santa Fe in 1698. At that time, he stated that his mother was Leonor Ruiz de Esparza, though these were surnames of a family to which she was rather indirectly related.[10]

On 1 February 1695, Arellano enlisted in Zacatecas as a colonist bound for New Mexico, with the Juan Páez Hurtado expedition. He was described as being sound of body, with straight black hair. Also on the expedition roster were Ursula Ramos de Arellano, listed as his sister, and Josefa Ramos, his niece.[11] Subsequent testimony in 1697 revealed that this was a fraudulent family, contrived to get the 344 pesos 3 1/2 tomines allotment given to the colonists. The two individuals in question were really Ursula and Josefa Reinoso, not related to Arellano in any way.[12]

The pay list for the Santa Fe presidio for the period from December 1696 to June 1697 indicates that Arellano was serving with the company.[13] The following year, when testimony was taken against Páez Hurtado, Arellano was described as a former member of his household and a partisan of Diego de Vargas in his struggle with Gov. Pedro Rodríguez Cubero. Arellano was accused of being the conduit through which the secret news that Vargas had been reappointed governor was to reach certain individuals, a charge Arellano corroborated.[14]

Arellano survived that tumultuous period and by 1702 was on duty in the Acoma-Zuni region. The following year, he got involved in a lawsuit with Sgt. Bartolomé Lobato over an Apache slave in Arellano's possession. Lobato requested delivery of an Apache woman owed him by Miguel Solá Cubero, nephew of the former governor, Pedro Rodríguez Cubero, and left with Cristóbal Arellano. Governor Vargas ordered her delivered within three days to Lobato.[15]

Arellano was alcalde mayor of Santa Cruz in 1704. On orders of Governor Cuervo y Valdés, he traded a dozen horses from the presidial herd at the Pecos trade fair, presumably before the Navajo expedition departed.[16] Arellano was serving as alcalde mayor of Santa Ana, Zia, and Jemez in the spring of 1716, when Gov. Félix Martínez began preparations for his campaign against the Hopi pueblos. In response to the governor's call, Arellano said that he could provide twelve Indians from Santa Ana, twenty-five from Zia, and twenty from Jemez as auxiliary troops.[17]

Fray Agustín de Colina

Fray Agustín de Colina, who had earlier been custos of the custody in the province of Zacatecas, was at La Junta de los Ríos with fray Joaquín de Hinojosa and another Franciscan in 1687, where they remained for a year and eight months. He served in various capacities in the mission field of El Paso between 1689 and 1692. Colina then spent several years as a missionary to the Jumanos, submitting a report in 1693 concerning the state of the missions at La Junta de los Ríos. Between 1703 and 1707, fray Agustín labored at Zia, Santa Ana, Bernalillo, Jemez, San Ildefonso, and Tesuque. In 1707 he was custos of the New Mexico missions and again serving in the El Paso area, at the Socorro Mission.[18]

Gerónimo Dirucaca

Gov. Diego de Vargas gave Gerónimo Dirucaca the cane signifying his selection as governor of Picuris Pueblo. By 1713 pueblo elders had taken it away from him. At that time, the former governor was brought to trial for challenging the teachings of the church, idolatry, witchcraft, and illicit sex.

Dirucaca admitted that, during Vargas's time, he had lived scandalously with a women and her three daughters and had had a child by one of them. Those activities had been investigated by the alcalde mayor at the time, his comrade-in-arms on the 1705 Navajo campaign, Cristóbal Arellano, but now he was falsely accused. From jail in Santa Fe, he informed Governor Flores Mogollón that he knew of the location of a silver mine. Having secured the promise of a pardon, a manacled Dirucaca led a party to a canyon near Picuris Pueblo, where they found four veins of ore, all of which appeared to contain silver. The charges against Dirucaca were dropped, though he was required to pay court costs and live in exile in the Tewa pueblo of his choosing.[19]

JOSEPH DOMÍNGUEZ [DE MENDOZA]

Joseph Domínguez de Mendoza was a New Mexico native, born around 1665, who survived the 1680 Pueblo Revolt. He was the son of Ana Velázquez and an unknown father, who was probably Tomé Domínguez de Mendoza II or his brother, Antonio.[20] In 1682 he married Juana López in the Real de San Lorenzo, at which point he was identified as Domínguez de Ace. At some time before his prenuptial investigations, he had been arrested in Mexico City for having someone else's mules in his possession, but he had gained his release.[21] Domínguez passed muster before Gov. Domingo Jironza Petrís de Cruzate on 14 November 1684. He stated that he was among those newly arrived whom Gov. Antonio de Otermín had sent to New Spain before the Pueblo Revolt to accompany outgoing Gov. Juan Francisco Treviño (1675–77) and await the arrival of the supply train at El Paso.

In the muster before Jironza in El Paso, Domínguez appeared with a harquebus, sword, shield, saddlebags, twenty balls of shot, one pound of gunpowder, one saddled horse, three remounts, and two mules.[22] He was listed among the veterans of the El Paso presidio in May 1684.[23] He passed muster before Governor Jironza in El Paso on 18 April 1686 and before Governor Reneros de Posada on 17 April 1687.[24]

Domínguez, a widower by 1690,[25] was an alferez during Vargas's 1692 reconquest of New Mexico. That year he rescued his sister, Juana, and five children (four daughters and a son).[26] By 1705 Domínguez was a captain and had remarried.[27] At that time, he was residing with his wife, Gerónima Varela de Perea, in Santa Cruz.[28] The couple had two children, María and Manuel. He served as alcalde mayor and *capitán a guerra* of Santo Domingo, San Felipe, and Cochiti from as early as 1714 and as late as 1719.[29] Domínguez served as *ayudante general* on Governor Martínez's 1716 Hopi campaign, during which he was in charge of the horses and cattle accompanying the expedition. When he passed muster for the campaign, he was fully armed and had five horses.[30] Domínguez died on 13 August 1720, in the massacre of the Villasur expedition.[31]

Seven years later, Domínguez's name came up during prenuptial investigations for the marriage of Francisco Rendón and Catarina Maese. A survivor of the disastrous battle against the Pawnees and French, Pedro Guillén, had returned with the tale that Domínguez had told him that Francisco Rendón was his illegitimate son. Another soldier, named Juan Luján, stated that the late Domínguez was also the father of Juan Antonio Domínguez. A number of Domínguez's friends, however, challenged these allegations, as did Francisco Rendón. Unfortunately the whole truth will probably never be known; the wedding did take place.[32]

Martín García

Martín García was born around 1655 in Sombrerete.[33] While assigned to the presidio of Santa Fe in 1702, he purchased property in town.[34] García was sentenced to four years in the presidio of Santa Rosa Cosihuiriáchic for mistreating New Mexico Indians. He apparently did not return to New Mexico.[35]

Juan Griego

It is unclear from the context whether this individual was one of the men-at-arms or a Pueblo auxiliary. If the former, he may have been one of two Hispanic Juan Griegos, aged twenty-nine and nineteen, respectively, who passed muster in 1680 at La Salineta. Both passed musters again in 1681 and 1684, one man in Ysleta del Sur and the other in the Real de San Lorenzo. In 1680 the younger man was accompanied by his mother, siblings, and another boy. The other Juan Griego was married, with a child.[36] One of the two Juans settled in the Albuquerque area, where he was living in 1718 when he sold some property in Santa Fe.[37] This man and his sister, Josefa, the wife of José Romero, were the children of Blas Griego and Inés Romero.[38] Juan had received a grant of land outside of Albuquerque in 1708. He was the widower of Antonia Varela when he married Juliana Sáiz, the daughter of Agustín Sáiz and Antonia Márquez, in Albuquerque in 1716.[39] Together they had at least two children: Joaquín, who married Francisco de la Luz Candelaria, and Tomasa.[40]

Alternatively he may have been the Juan Griego who was a Pueblo leader from San Juan in the 1696 revolt.[41] Two years earlier, this man was described as the principal war captain.[42]

Alejo Gutiérrez

Alejo Gutiérrez, the son of New Mexico natives Roque Gutiérrez and María de Tapia, was the brother of Juan Roque

Gutiérrez, who also participated on the 1705 Navajo campaign.⁴³ On 11 September 1684, his mother, already a widow, passed muster in El Paso. She and the other five members of her household were in abject poverty.⁴⁴ In addition to her sons, Alejo and Juan Roque, there were at least two sisters, María and Isabel.

Gutiérrez's marriage to María Hurtado was investigated in 1699. They had a daughter, Inés. Alejo and his wife were associated with the cofradia of the Holy Sacrament, and he was a member of the Third Order of St. Francis.⁴⁵ He acquired property in Santa Fe and was still serving with the presidio as late as 1713.⁴⁶ He died after 1727, probably in Bernalillo.⁴⁷

Juan Roque Gutiérrez

Born in New Mexico around 1671, Juan Roque Gutiérrez was the son of Roque Gutiérrez and María de Tapia and the brother of Alejo.⁴⁸ He had joined the El Paso presidio company by the time of his marriage investigation in January 1690. His petition to marry María García, the daughter of the Conchos presidio soldier and Zacatecas native Juan García and the New Mexico native Margarita Márquez, was opposed by Antonia Martín. She stated that Juan had deflowered her. He admitted that what Antonia had stated was true, that he had promised to marry her, and that he had perjured himself because the alcalde, José Téllez Girón, had threatened to garrote him if he refused to marry María García. Gov. Diego de Vargas intervened in the case and ordered Juan to marry Antonia Martín. The wedding was celebrated on 18 February.⁴⁹ The union produced a daughter, Josefa, who married Diego Gallegos, son of José Gallegos and Catarina Hurtado, in 1709.⁵⁰

In 1702 Gutiérrez was still assigned to the presidial company in El Paso,⁵¹ but on 16 April 1705, he was in Santa Fe to give his opinion about an impending expedition against the Navajos.[52] He did not, however, pass muster with the citizens on 20–22 April 1705.[53]

In April 1706, Governor Cuervo sent Maestre de campo Gutiérrez to Zuni, in command of a squadron of eight soldiers.[54] At that time, the Hopis were waging a bitter war against the Zunis, who had angered them by accepting Christianity. Together with Zuni allies, Gutiérrez and his men were to maintain a defensive position. In May Gutiérrez, his men, and his Zuni allies carried out a raid against the Hopis, during which they managed to carry off sixty animals and kill two of the enemy.

Inspired by this success, Gutiérrez requested reinforcements from the governor so that he could lead a second foray. In response Cuervo dispatched Capt. Tomás López Holguín with a squadron of soldiers. After patrolling in defense of Zuni through the summer, Gutiérrez led another expedition to Hopi. Led by the Zunis, the party arrived one night at the Tiwa pueblo, located between Walpi and Oraibi on a high mesa, and laid siege to the pueblo. Before dawn an Indian woman coming down for water saw the troops creeping up to the pueblo and alerted her people.

After a brief skirmish, the Tiwas requested peace, offering one of their own as a hostage, and the soldiers began to come back down off the mesa. Before they were halfway down, some Tanos arrived to assist the besieged Tiwas. They fell on the soldiers so aggressively that they killed three and wounded many; all were at risk of losing their lives. The Indians managed to get some guns away from the troops and forced them to flee. Gutiérrez ordered the Tiwa hostage shot at Awatovi and then returned to Zuni.[55] Gutiérrez must have left the Zuni area soon after these events; in 1707, he was an alcalde in Santa Fe.[56] That year a reddish-colored horse provided to Gutiérrez for use on the Navajo campaign was safely returned to the governor.[57] Juan Roque Gutiérrez died, probably in Bernalillo, by October 1709.[58]

MIGUEL DE HERRERA

Miguel de Herrera was born in New Mexico around 1671 to Capt. Juan de Herrera and Ana López [del Castillo]. He took the place of Antonio de Avalos in the presidial company of El Paso in 1689.[59] The following year, he married Mariana García at Guadalupe del Paso.[60] The couple had a daughter, María, who married Diego Trujillo, son of Sgt. Cristóbal Trujillo and Micaela Archuleta, in Santa Cruz in 1709. Their son Miguel married Antonia Trujillo, daughter of Capt. José Trujillo and Antonia Luján, in 1716.[61] Herrera eventually married again. His second wife, Antonia de Archuleta, bore him four children: Miguel, Casilda, Juan Antonio, and probably José.[62]

As late as 1702, Herrera was still assigned to the El Paso presidio.[63] As a military leader, he gave a negative opinion about an expedition against the Navajos in April 1705 and apparently did not participate.[64] Herrera was still serving at the Santa Fe presidio in 1710.[65] Diego Velasco murdered Herrera in 1712.[66]

TOMÁS LÓPEZ HOLGUÍN

Tomás López Holguín was likely the son of Capt. Juan Holguín and María Luján.[67] He enlisted in the El Paso presidio in 1691.[68] In 1692 he saw the bones of Antonio Gómez, who had been slain at Zia five years earlier. In March 1694, Holguín was a *cabo* during the siege of Black Mesa.[69] Holguín's place in the El Paso company was taken in 1698, for some unexplained reason. He was a captain assigned to the presidio of Santa Fe by 1706. Holguín led a squadron of soldiers that went to Zuni as reinforcements for Juan Roque Gutiérrez that summer and participated in the Hopi campaigns of the following year.[70]

Holguín was alcalde mayor of Santa Cruz when he stated his opinion about a proposed campaign against the Navajos in 1713. The Franciscan priest at San Ildefonso had reported that Navajos had stolen livestock, and Governor Flores Mogollón sought advice from the most experienced military men. Holguín called for an investigation to determine whether the Navajos were really the guilty parties and suggested delaying action until instructions could be sent for and received from the viceroy in Mexico City.[71] During another junta of war, in July 1714, he offered his insight into the wisdom of permitting Indians to continue their traditional customs. Holguín expressed the opinion that Pueblos should not be allowed to paint themselves with vermillion or wear feathers on their heads or ears when they went inside a church, because this was a declared abuse like the use of kivas. Furthermore they should enter and leave their pueblos only by the camino real. Doing otherwise frightened travelers, who mistook the Pueblos for Apaches. Holguín stated that these strictures should be enforced by the alcaldes mayores. Surprisingly the Franciscans did not concur in this opinion.[72]

A Tomás Holguín was married to Ursula Gómez at that time, and he may be the same individual described here. This man, or another by the same name, was married to María de la Cruz, who was deceased by 1715. While it is somewhat unclear, there seems to have been only one Tomás Holguín at this time. Their son, Antonio, underwent prenuptial investigations to wed Micaela de Moraga, daughter of Alonso de Moraga and Juana de Leyba, in 1707 in Socorro.[73]

Holguín served as second-in-command on Governor Martínez's 1716 Hopi campaign, at which time he was alcalde mayor of Santa Cruz. He passed muster with all the necessary weapons and seven horses. Following the governor's orders, Holguín readied seventy of the one hundred presidial soldiers to take the field on 16 August. Once in the theater of operations, Holguín led a force of sixty soldiers and one hundred Indian allies in a raid on the milpas, fields, and mesa top at Walpi.[74]

The following year, Holguín got caught up in the seemingly inevitable controversy that surrounded the change of administration from one governor to the next. Fearing imprisonment by Antonio Valverde Cosío, who had been sent to Santa Fe to sort out the difficulty between Martínez and Flores Mogollón, López Holguín sought asylum in the church in Santa Fe. There he composed several letters to the viceroy of New Spain, the Marqués de Valero, in which he protested his innocence in the whole affair. He stated that he was a loyal servant of the crown and that Martínez had forced the presidial soldiers to sign statements against Flores Mogollón, and that this would be corroborated by Cristóbal de la Serna, who was in Mexico City, and by Roque Madrid, who had also sought asylum in the church in Santa Fe.[75] In the event, Serna denied everything Holguín and Madrid stated, suggesting that the letters were forgeries.[76]

In giving his opinion during a junta of war in August 1719, he stated that he had served the crown in New Mexico for thirty years.[77] In June 1720 he was on inactive duty but joined the Villasur expedition as maestre de campo. He died on 13 August 1720 in the massacre.[78]

In the investigation of Gov. Antonio Valverde Cosío in the aftermath of the disaster, some testimony revealed that Holguín had disagreed with Villasur about the proper course of action after encountering the French and Indian enemies. Holguín counseled continued retreat and stated that the encampment Villasur had selected was indefensible, which events proved to be the case.[79]

In his own defense, Valverde blamed Holguín, reputed to be the most experienced military man in the province at the time, for the massacre. He held Holguín responsible for leaving the camp undefended.[80]

Fray Francisco Jiménez

Fray Francisco Jiménez was a native of Ayamonte, in southwestern Spain. He professed in the Franciscan Order on 1 September 1690. He was president and missionary of San Gerónimo de Taos in 1706. In Picuris Pueblo in August of that year, he received sixty-two apostates brought back from El Cuartelejo by order of Gov. Cuervo y Valdés. In 1707 he was vice-custos and still assigned to Taos.[81]

Roque Madrid

Born around 1644 in New Mexico, to Francisco Madrid II and Sebastiana Ruíz de Cáceres,[82] Roque Madrid and his brother Lorenzo played leading roles in late-seventeenth- and early-eighteenth–century New Mexico. His hacienda was located near the Arroyo de San Marcos, a little less than 2 leagues from Santa Fe.[83] During the retreat from the Pueblo Revolt, on 14 September 1680, at the campsite of Fray Cristóbal, Roque Madrid concurred with the consensus about how the refugees should proceed; it was his counsel that they should continue downriver to the El Paso area, rather than try to regroup on the run.[84] When he passed muster on 29 September at La Salineta, he was described as a captain with three skinny horses, two thin mules, the full complement of personal weapons, a wife, and two small children. He stated that the enemy had robbed his house and that he was in extreme poverty.[85]

The following year, he enlisted as a settler, now described as a tall, slim man of dark complexion, with a grey beard and thick black hair. He received a ploughshare, an axe, and four hoes.[86] Madrid participated in Otermín's ill-starred attempted reconquest of the province during the winter of 1681–82. He accompanied Juan Domínguez de Mendoza on the northern leg of the expedition, which went beyond vanquished Isleta as far as Cochiti.[87] In many respects this dramatic foray deep into enemy-held territory foreshadowed the actions Madrid was to take throughout his career.

The certification for presidial service from 17 April 1683 to 17 April 1684 did not include Roque Madrid.[88] Nevertheless in September he was listed among the veterans of the El Paso presidio, as captain of the presidio and *sargento mayor*.[89] When the El Paso presidial troops were sent to Casas Grandes, as a response to the May 1684 Suma revolt, Madrid joined forces with two stalwart frontier captains, Juan Fernández de la Fuente and Francisco Ramírez de Salazar, in a September campaign directed at stopping an alliance of Apaches, Janos, and Mansos against the Spaniards. The following year, he gave a summary of his recent activities while testifying in behalf of New Mexico governor Jironza.

Madrid stated that he had gone out on 10 forays during Jironza's term and provided some details about half of them. First he led 25 men from the El Paso presidio on a retaliatory raid against Apaches who had taken livestock from Ysleta and Socorro. He and his men had routed the enemy at Cerro Agujerado, killing a few. Second he had led an escort of 25 men to safeguard the supplies sent to the Franciscans and New Mexico colonists during a time of general rebellion. Third Madrid had joined the governor in the field against the Mansos, destroying their rancherias. Fourth he led a large force, consisting of 50 presidial soldiers and 170 Indian allies on a punitive raid against the Apaches. When they finally found the enemy, the troops were badly mauled, suffering many wounded, and had to withdraw. A second battle produced a victory, but only after a day-long struggle. Finally, after Indians overran an escort, Madrid accompanied Jironza on another campaign that resulted in some Indians killed and the women and children taken prisoner.[90] Madrid mustered before Governor Jironza in El Paso on 18 April 1686 as captain, cabo, and caudillo and before Governor Reneros de Posada on 17 April 1687 as sargento mayor.[91]

In the late summer of 1692, Gov. Diego de Vargas assigned Madrid the trusted position of vanguard for the impending reconquest of New Mexico. On 16 August 1692, Roque Madrid led the first troops, consisting of three squadrons with the expedition's supplies and livestock, out of El Paso. Vargas remained in El Paso awaiting reinforcements from New Biscay.[92]

Vargas selected Madrid for a similarly important role in the 1693 recolonizing venture. The governor gave him command over all of the soldiers on the expedition, while entrusting overall direction to his lieutenant governor, Luis Granillo.[93] In September of that year, Madrid was granted land near Santa Fe, bounded by Pueblo Quemado and Ojo Fresco, belonging to his grandfather and father, as well as some additional land, for his loyal service to the crown.[94]

During his years of service with Vargas, Madrid was singled out for the special task of provisioning the troops with maize. In a sense, he acted as a specialized quartermaster, charged with the procurement, transport, and distribution of maize to the hungry men-at-arms. On no fewer than half a dozen separate occasions over the years, Vargas dispatched Madrid to secure maize for the soldiers.[95] Madrid was also pressed into service as an interpreter at times. He stated that he understood and spoke the language of Pecos Pueblo, which was Towa, although he apparently had some reservations about his ability to translate it. He expressed no such reluctance to act as an interpreter of Keresan, perhaps a result of living in close proximity to San Marcos Pueblo.[96]

His supply duties and translating chores notwithstanding, Madrid was always in the forefront on the field of battle. Of the numerous examples, the assault on the mesa of Cochiti on 16 April 1694 stands out. Madrid and the Indian Bartolomé Ojeda led a column of forty Spaniards and one hundred Indian allies up the main road to the mesa. Two other columns joined them in the assault.

In the attack on the mesa, seven of the defenders perished and another died from burns received when the Indian allies set fire to the homes. The Spaniards captured 342 people and executed 13 leaders. The victors divided 70 horses and mules, 900 sheep, clothing, and foodstuff.[97]

Vargas ordered Madrid to call in all the Franciscans to Santa Fe for their protection in June 1696. Madrid responded to the crisis by sending horses to Vargas, along with the news that San Cristóbal Pueblo, the Keres nation, the Apaches, the Hopis, and the Pecos had risen against the Spaniards. The outbreak of the second Pueblo revolt in June 1696 found Lt. general Roque Madrid coming to the defense of his home in Santa Cruz, where he was alcalde mayor and capitán a guerra. By October he was able to report that Juan Chillo and Juan Griego, two of the rebel leaders, had surrendered and that many of the Picuris had fled the province.[98]

Roque Madrid had prospered and grown in stature under the administration of Diego de Vargas. When Vargas's successor, Pedro Rodríguez Cubero, arrived in July 1697, he must have been numbered among the governor's backers. Yet Madrid was a native New Mexican and may have harbored resentment against the influence of the outsiders in Vargas's household.

In February 1699, he delivered scathing testimony against Antonio Valverde Cosío, a Spaniard from the province of Santander, who had cast his lot with Vargas while engaged in commerce in Sombrerete in 1693. Valverde was seeking confirmation at court in Madrid for his grant of the title of captain of the El Paso presidio. Among the damning charges were accusations of living in concubinage, mocking the Laws of the Indies, lack of experience, and slaving. Later Vargas's attorney in Mexico City, José de Ledesma, claimed that Madrid had been forced to sign the statement against Valverde. Whatever the case, evidence exists to suggest a lasting enmity between Madrid and Valverde that transcended this episode.[99]

Madrid was officially part of the presidial company of El Paso as late as 1700.[100] As 1707 came to a close, he was living in Santa Cruz and defending himself against serious charges leveled by the Indians of San Juan Pueblo, who accused him of abusing them and extorting from them.[101]

He had further legal difficulty in 1708, while still living in Santa Cruz, when he became embroiled in a lawsuit with Silvestre Pacheco over some land south of Santa Fe, held jointly by the Pachecos and the Madrids before the Pueblo Revolt. The two men eventually compromised and exchanged some land.[102]

Roque Madrid was called on to lead troops against the Navajos when they raided near Santa Clara Pueblo and fighting broke out again in February 1709. He led another campaign in December 1709.[103] All the while he either served various terms as alcalde mayor of Santa Cruz through 1712 or continuously held the office, because his name appears frequently in the historical record in that capacity. In January of that year, he oversaw the distribution of tools to the residents of Santa Cruz by the governor, the Marqués de la Peñuela.[104] That same year Madrid and several other citizens of Santa Cruz petitioned for permission to move to the site of Yunque-Yunque on the Rio Grande, but the request was denied for fear of the abandonment of Santa Cruz.[105] Beginning in 1713, he was assigned to the presidial company in Santa Fe.[106] In March 1714, he again led operations against the Navajos and that summer participated in a junta of war concerning the advisability of launching a campaign against the Faraón Apaches.[107] The following winter, as one of the most experienced soldiers in the kingdom, he advised Governor Flores Mogollón in another junta of war.[108] He was to have participated in Páez Hurtado's 1715 Apache campaign, but was ill with flux.[109] Madrid continued his presidial service until at least the summer of 1716, when he would have been about seventy-two years old. At that time, he participated in Governor Martínez's Hopi campaign. Madrid passed muster as maestre de campo, but he was only fourth-in-command behind Governor Martínez, Mre. de campo Tomás López Holguín, and Alfonso Rael de Aguilar. Madrid was fully armed and had four horses for the campaign, but lacked a cuera, the protective leather jacket.[110]

The previous February, Roque Madrid married Josefa Durán.[111] He was the widower of Juana de Arvid [Arvizu y Gamboa], who had died in late 1713. He and Juana had several children: Pedro, Matías, José, and Josefa, wife of Cristóbal de la Serna. Josefa Durán was herself the widow of Agustín Griego. Her husband notwithstanding, Josefa had been Roque's mistress for thirty-eight years by that time (according to one witness). She had borne him at least three children: Antonia, Julián, and Miguel Angel.[112]

After a distinguished career and having safely passed the venerable age of seventy, Madrid found himself embroiled in the struggle between Ignacio Flores Mogollón and Félix Martínez. In the summer of 1717, he and his long-time comrade in arms, Tomás

López Holguín, had sought asylum in the church in Santa Fe. Madrid felt contempt for Valverde, who had come to Santa Fe to resolve the dispute. Writing to the viceroy, Madrid stated that every time Valverde came to Santa Fe it was to do harm to the soldiers. He added that he had ignorantly signed documents condemning Flores Mogollón at the bidding of Martínez, whose only aim was vengeance. He meant no harm to a superior and remained his majesty's loyal servant.[113] As Christmas was approaching, Madrid and the rest of the Santa Fe presidial soldiers received word of the viceroy's decision. On 20 December 1717, Governor Valverde Cosío read them their pardon. Among those present was Roque Madrid.[114] He was dead by 1723.[115]

José [López] Naranjo

José Naranjo was born around 1670. He may have been one of the four Indians Governor Otermín questioned in December 1681, after the Pueblo Revolt. At that time a José, who could speak Spanish, was interrogated, along with Pedro Naranjo. In October 1692, he was sent to talk with Diego de Vargas at Taos and identified himself as Josefillo, El Español. In later documents he is variously described as black, mulatto, or Indian.[116]

In June 1696, while living in Santa Cruz, Naranjo learned that an Indian uprising was imminent and warned the alcalde mayor, Roque Madrid. Naranjo was instrumental in assisting Governor Rodríguez Cubero to persuade the Keresans to come down from Enchanted Mesa, north of Acoma, and in establishing Laguna Pueblo. The following year, Naranjo, his wife, and three other, unnamed people received goods at the general distribution in Santa Fe.[117]

Naranjo eventually became even more assimilated with the Spaniards and was serving as alcalde mayor of Halona by 1700. He was still acting in that capacity in 1702, when Juan de Ulibarrí

23 / Painting of José de Naranjo, by Claudine Morrow, 1968. (Courtesy of Indian Pueblo Cultural Museum, Albuquerque.)

investigated unrest at Laguna, Acoma, and Zuni pueblos.[118] On one of his trips to the area, Naranjo left his name carved on Inscription Rock at El Morro. By 1704 he was Vargas's principal scout and captain of the Indian allies. He also scouted for Ulibarrí's 1706 expedition to El Cuartelejo.[119]

José Naranjo owned property at La Vega, near present-day Española. A census of Santa Cruz conducted in 1707 listed Naranjo, his wife, and five additional family members. Naranjo was married to Catalina Luján, one of the natural daughters of Matías Luján of Santa Cruz. José and Catalina produced at least one child whose name is known, José Antonio. He married Juana Márquez, daughter of Mexico City native Diego Márquez and María de Palacios, in 1719.[120]

In 1709 Naranjo served with Roque Madrid on another campaign. Because of his vital roll as Indian leader and interpreter, he may well have served in all three expeditions that the Marqués de la Peñuela ordered into the field that year.

In 1714 he participated in a council of war as principal Indian war captain.[121] Naranjo also led the scouts and 150 Pueblo auxiliaries from Pecos, San Juan, Nambe, San Ildefonso, Santa Clara, Pojoaque, Tesuque, Taos, and Picuris on Juan Páez Hurtado's 1715 Apache campaign.[122] He served in a similar role on Governor Valverde's Comanche and Ute campaign in 1719.[123] Naranjo had the dubious honor of being named chief scout on the 1720 Pedro de Villasur expedition, which resulted in his death.[124]

CRISTÓBAL DE LA SERNA

Cristóbal de la Serna, age 19, married Josefa Madrid, daughter of Roque Madrid and Juana de Arvid, at Guadalupe del Paso in 1694. He was the son of Felipe de la Serna and Isabel López.[125] Serna and his wife had at least two daughters: María and

Sebastiana. María wed Nicolás Jacinto, son of Alejo Martín and María de la Rocha, in 1712.[126] Sebastiana became the wife of Lorenzo Griego, son of Agustín Griego and Josefa Durán, in 1715.[127] Cristóbal and Josefa also had two sons: Juan and Sebastián. Two of Cristóbal's sisters also married into the Madrid family. Isabel married Pedro Madrid in El Paso in 1689, and Antonia married Matías Madrid there in 1696.

Cristóbal went off active-duty status with the presidial company of El Paso in April 1700.[128] In 1706 he was a squad leader and later a captain with the Santa Fe presidio.[129] The following September, the sorrel-colored horse that Cuervo y Valdés had provided for his use on the Navajo campaign was returned to the governor.[130] His petition to the Marqués de la Peñuela for land was granted on 8 April 1710. Serna's grant was south of Taos Pueblo and was one of the few land grants in the area at the time.[131]

In 1712, amid a swirl of lawsuits relating to presidial matters, Gov. Juan Ignacio Flores Mogollón removed Félix Martínez as captain of the Santa Fe presidio, replacing him with Serna. He led an expedition against the Navajos in 1713 and again in 1716, when he also commanded several operations against Utes and Comanches, defeating them north of Taos and taking many prisoners. Despite their differences, Martínez called on Serna to play a major role in the Hopi campaign that summer. At the time, he passed muster with all the necessary weapons and 5 horses. Serna led 60 soldiers and 150 Indians in the assault on the mesa-top strongholds of Moshonavi and Shongopavi.[132]

Early in 1717, as a captain on inactive-duty status, Serna accompanied Félix Martínez and Ignacio Flores Mogollón to Mexico City, as part of a delegation from New Mexico that included an Indian captain named Cristóbal Mariquita, a Tewa who had been named lieutenant governor of all the Pueblos of New Mexico by the former viceroy of New Spain, the Duque de Alburquerque.[133]

Serna testified that the soldiers of the Santa Fe presidio had asked Martínez to prevent Flores Mogollón from leaving New Mexico until accounts between the soldiers and the former governor could be settled. He added that the soldiers were adamantly opposed to Antonio Valverde Cosío being named governor. They held him personally responsible for the loss of a year's salary (more than 43,000 pesos) during the administration of the interim governor, Francisco Cuervo y Valdés.[134] On 3 June 1717, Martínez was reinstated.

Serna died on 13 August 1720, a member of the ill-fated Villasur expedition.[135] Therefore he did not apply for a land grant in 1748 in the Taos Valley, as Chavez states; rather the applicant was Cristóbal Torres, a former comrade-in-arms of Serna.[136]

ANTONIO TAFOYA ALTAMIRANO

Antonio Tafoya Altamirano was born to Juan de Tafoya Altamirano de Estrada and Felipa Jaguada de Ulloa sometime between 1672 and 1679, one of three brothers in a family from Tlalpujahua, Michoacán, where Diego de Vargas served earlier in his career.[137] He and his brothers, Cristóbal and Juan, were among a number of people from Tlalpujahua who came to New Mexico while Vargas was governor. Before that Tafoya served with the presidial company of Cuencamé.[138] After rejoining Vargas in Santa Fe in 1695, Tafoya married María Luisa Godines, the widow of Alonso García de Noriega II.[139] The couple had two known sons and three daughters: Cristóbal, Felipe, Lutgarda, María Rosa, and Juana.[140]

In addition to participating in the 1705 Roque Madrid expedition, Tafoya also went on another campaign to Navajo country in the winter of 1708–9 and was a cabo on Juan Páez Hurtado's 1715 Apache campaign.[141] He held the same rank when he passed muster with all the necessary weapons and five horses the following year, as a participant in the Hopi campaign.[142] In 1718 Tafoya purchased property in Santa Fe.[143] Gov. Juan Domingo Bustamante ordered him to go on campaign against the Apaches of the Ladron and Sandia mountains with 50 soldiers and 150 Indian allies in June 1724.[144]

Antonio Tafoya and Carlos de Mirabal, who were living in La Cañada de Santa Clara, in the jurisdiction of Santa Cruz, ran afoul of the law in 1735. The two men were encroaching on the territory of Santa Clara Pueblo and one of its citizens. Tafoya and Mirabal were keeping in their house the Apache wife of one Antonio, an Indian from Santa Clara. Juan Lorenzo de Valdés, acting for Alcalde mayor Juan Esteban García de Noriega, attempted to return the woman to Santa Clara, but they refused to give her up, saying that her husband had left her there. Valdés persisted, and the woman was taken from their home.

In addition to the offense of disobedience, Tafoya and Mirabal were accused of planting on their farm. They had been expressly forbidden to do so by an edict from Governor Bustamante and an order from Gov. Gervasio Cruzat y Góngora. Juan Páez Hurtado adjudicated the case and reported his findings to Governor Cruzat y Góngora. The governor sentenced Tafoya and Mirabal for disobedience and illegal planting.[145]

After a long career in the royal service, Tafoya lost his eyesight and retired in 1747. Two years earlier, he had testified about the 1705 campaign, stating that the Spanish forces, consisting of soldiers, settlers, and Indian allies, had numbered four hundred. He further stated that on that occasion he had seen some five hundred Navajos, young and old. He stated that this expedition had entered Navajo country by way of the Sierra de las Grullas and exited by way of Los Pedernales, near Abiquiu.[146]

Tafoya died on 17 Feb. 1753, at which time he was an alferez on reserve status. This individual is not to be confused with his nephew of the same name, who owned land near Santa Cruz and Santa Clara Pueblo.[147]

Mateo Trujillo

Mateo Trujillo was a native of New Mexico, born around 1664.[148] Trujillo passed muster in El Paso on 23 September 1681. At the time, he was described as a married man who was tall and slender, of very dark complexion, with thick, straight hair. He enlisted as a settler and was given the equivalent of 250 pesos in goods, including a plow, axe, and four hoes.[149]

Trujillo miraculously escaped death in the 1696 Pueblo revolt. He received a land grant in the area south of Santa Clara Pueblo and very near San Ildefonso in 1700. He bought property in Santa Fe in 1703 and sold lots and a house in 1722. His wife was María de Tapia, widow of Alonso Romero. The couple had three known children: Juana, Francisco, and Agustín.[150] Agustín underwent prenuptial investigations in 1696 to marry Micaela Martín, the widow of Cristóbal Luján and daughter of Capt. Pedro Martín and Juana de Argüello.[151] Mateo Trujillo survived until at least 1728, when he sold his holdings near San Ildefonso.[152]

Antonio de Ulibarrí

Antonio de Ulibarrí was probably born around 1682, in San Luis de la Paz, Guanajuato, to José Enríquez de los Reyes and María de Hinojos.[153] His relationship to Juan de Ulibarrí is unclear, having been noted as both brother and son, as is his use of the surname Ulibarrí. He was married to María Durán y Chaves by 1711. Apparently the couple had no children of their own, but raised Rosa de Armijo in their home. Rosa eventually sued Ulibarrí for the dowry belonging to his wife.[154]

Ulibarrí acted in the capacity of legal representative of the soldiers of the Santa Fe presidio in their lawsuit against Cuervo y Valdés, filing an appeal against the ruling in favor of the former governor. From 1714 he was alcalde of Laguna, Acoma, and Zuni.[155]

When Gov. Juan Páez Hurtado reviewed the troops for his 1715 Apache campaign, Ulibarrí passed muster in Picuris Pueblo as a settler from Albuquerque.[156] The following summer, he participated in Gov. Félix Martínez's campaign against the Hopi pueblos. He was listed among the citizens of Santa Fe and passed muster with all the necessary weapons, five horses and, two mules. Only a protective leather coat was missing from his kit.[157]

In October 1716, Ulibarrí sued Cristóbal Martín and his mother, Antonia de Moraga, for possession of land in Chimayó that he had purchased from his brother, Juan de Ulibarrí.[158] Juan had acquired the land from José de Castellanos. Governor Martínez found in favor of Moraga and her son. In April 1727, Ulibarrí sold a house and land in Santa Fe to María de Tafoya.[159] By 1731 he was serving as alcalde mayor of Santa Fe. Ulibarrí registered a parcel of uncultivated land early in 1735, with the approval of Juan Páez Hurtado, who was acting in the governor's stead while he was absent on an inspection tour in the El Paso area.[160] Ulibarrí's wife died, probably around March 1724, and he married Teresa Antonia Rael de Aguilar. Together they had a daughter named Feliciana, who became the wife of Juan de Anaya in 1748.

In 1745 Ulibarrí gave testimony about a campaign to the Navajo country in 1706. The details of his account so closely match those recorded in the journal of Roque Madrid's 1705 expedition that it seems logical that over time he had become confused about the correct date of the action. Only his insistence that there were no rivers is at odds with the campaign journal.

According to Ulibarrí, an unspecified number of soldiers and citizens entered Navajo country by way of Picuris Pueblo, traveling as far as Los Peñoles, in the center of their territory. He stated that Los Peñoles was 40 leagues from Picuris Pueblo. There were no pueblos in that country, which was full of mesas and cañadas. The land was pleasant with flowers, though they found no rivers. They did, however, find some springs and rain-fed water holes. As far as Los Peñoles, they saw some 200 Indians. Without doubt, opined Ulibarrí, there were many more on the mesas, where they had their houses of stone and wood, although his observation about houses could relate to his second campaign in October 1716. The Spaniards saw some small herds of sheep, from which they took about fifty head. In all of the province of the Navajos, Ulibarrí found no river suitable for irrigating their fields, which were dry-farmed. The expedition returned by way of Zia Pueblo.[161] Ulibarrí died on 2 November 1762.[162]

Juan de Ulibarrí

Juan de Ulibarrí came to New Mexico at the time of the Reconquest. He stated that he was born around 1670, in San Luis Potosí.[163] Only one baptismal record for a Juan de Ulibarrí for that year in San Luis Potosí has been found. On 8 March 1670 the baptism was recorded for Juan de Ulibarrí, the mulatto son of María de Ulibarrí, an unmarried mulatta slave of María de Ulibarrí, an unmarried Spanish woman who was a citizen of San Luis Potosí and the daughter of Capt. Juan de Ulibarrí. The godfather was a mestizo, Antonio Rodríguez, also a citizen of San Luis Potosí. Two years earlier, the same slave named María de Ulibarrí gave birth to another son, José. As the son of a slave, Juan would have been born into slavery. If this individual was the same man who came to New Mexico and became a general, his rise from slavery was a truly remarkable one. If so, at present it is not known how he might have acquired his manumission.[164] It is always possible and, indeed, likely that there were two men named Juan de Ulibarrí who came to New Mexico at about the same time, and their identities have been merged into one.

At the time of the 1696 Pueblo revolt, Ulibarrí was one of the military leaders of the colony. Gov. Pedro Rodríguez Cubero named him alcalde mayor and captain of the presidio of El Paso, where he was serving in 1699.[165] Within two years, he left his name carved in Inscription Rock, at El Morro. In 1702 Governor Rodríguez Cubero dispatched him to the Zuni area to investigate a plot against the Spaniards.[166]

Ulibarrí led an expedition to El Cuartelejo in 1706–7 that returned Picuris Indians, who had been living among the Apaches, to their pueblo. This operation was a part of Governor Cuervo y Valdés's plan to protect and unite the Pueblos against the Navajos and Apaches. He authorized fifty soldiers and one hundred Indian allies, but Ulibarrí actually departed with only forty men-at-arms (twenty-eight soldiers and twelve citizen militiamen), together with the stated number of Indians.[167]

At the time of his trip to El Cuartelejo, he was married to Juana Hurtado. By early 1709, he was alcalde mayor and capitán a guerra of Santa Cruz.[168] Later that year, while in Santa Fe, he petitioned for a land grant in the Albuquerque area.[169] He also denounced as abandoned a mine called Santa Rosa in the *cerrillos* de San Marcos that had been worked by Governor Rodríguez Cubero.[170] At that time, Ulibarrí was described as "sargento mayor, regidor y procurador" of New Mexico and was acting in the capacity of secretary of government and war. The following January, he registered another mine, which he named San Miguel Arcángel, located 15 to 16 leagues from Santa Fe.[171] In November 1711, General and Sargento mayor Ulibarrí was back in the El Paso area, under the command of Antonio Valverde Cosío.[172] Soon thereafter authorities in Mexico City summoned him to defend himself against charges leveled by the Tafoya brothers of New Mexico. The Tafoyas were among a group of men from Tlalpujahua in highland Michoacán who followed Diego de Vargas to New Mexico to serve under his command.

Ulibarrí's second wife, Francisca de Mizquía, petitioned for his release that year.[173] Whatever the outcome of her entreaty, Ulibarrí never returned to New Mexico, and she must have died soon thereafter. Juan died and was buried in Mexico City on 28 October 1716. At the time, he was living on the Calle de la Encarnación and married to another woman, Gertrudis Josefa de Ojeda.[174]

Juan de Zamora

Little is known of Juan de Zamora. A man by that name, born around 1655, stated that he was a New Mexico native on 6 October 1681, when he passed muster in El Paso before Governor Otermín. He was described as being a married man of good stature, his face scared by smallpox, with blond hair and beard. Enlisting as a settler, he was issued the equivalent of 250 pesos in goods.[175]

He may have been the same Juan de Zamora who was living with his wife, María de la Vega, and children in Santa Cruz de la Cañada in 1696. He was presumed killed between Cochiti and Santo Domingo that year, in the outbreak of the second Pueblo revolt, though his body was never recovered.[176] The following year, María and her children, Josefa, María, and Antonio, participated in the distribution of supplies in Santa Fe.[177]

Abbreviations

AASF	Archives of the Archdiocese of Santa Fe, Santa Fe, New Mexico
AGI	Archivo General de Indias, Seville, Spain
AGN	Archivo General de la Nación, Mexico City, Mexico
BNM	Biblioteca Nacional de México, Mexico City, Mexico
BNMad.	Biblioteca Nacional de Madrid, Madrid, Spain
BYU	Brigham Young University, Spanish New Mexico Collection
LDS	Church of Jesus Christ of Latter-day Saints, Genealogical Library, Microfilm
SANM	New Mexico State Records Center and Archives, Santa Fe, New Mexico
ZCCL	Zacatecas Collection, Clements Library, University of Michigan, Ann Arbor, Michigan

Notes

Preface

1. Frank D. Reeve, "Navajo-Spanish Wars, 1680–1720," NMHR 33 (1958): 218–21.
2. Frank McNitt. *Navajo Wars: Military Campaigns, Slave Raids, and Reprisals* (Albuquerque, 1972), 20–22.

Introduction

1. Francisco Cuervo y Valdés to the Duque de Alburquerque, Santa Fe, 7 May 1705, AGN Provincias Internas, 36:5. Silvestre Vélez de Escalante, Extracto de noticias, BNM 3:1. The authors express their appreciation to Eleanor B. Adams for permission to consult her unpublished transcription of the Extracto de noticias.
2. Duque de Alburquerque, Testimony, Mexico City, 28 Feb. 1706, SANM II:122. Ovidio Casado Fuente, *Don Francisco Cuerbo y Valdés, gobernador de Nuevo México, fundador de la ciudad de Albuquerque* (Oviedo, 1983), 34. Edward K. Flagler, "Defensive Policy and Indian Relations in New Mexico During the Tenure of Governor Francisco Cuervo y Valdés, 1705–1707," *Revista Española de Antropología Americana* 22 (1992): 92.
3. Fray Juan de Tagle, Certification, Santa Fe, 17 Oct. 1705, AGN Provincias Internas, 35:6. Copies in AGI Guadalajara, 116, and BNM 5:10. Fray Juan Alvarez, Certification, Santa Fe, 4 May 1705, AGN Provincias Internas, 36:5.
4. Reeve, "Navaho-Spanish Wars," 216. Vélez de Escalante, Extracto de noticias. Flagler, "Defensive Policy," 94. Juan de Dios Lucero de Godoy, Campaign journal, Encinillas, 13 Apr. 1705, SANM II:110.
5. Francisco Cuervo y Valdés, Muster, Santa Fe, 20 Apr. 1705, SANM II:110. Casado Fuente, "Don Francisco Cuerbo y Valdés," 43–44.

131

6. Juan de Ulibarrí, Muster, Bernalillo, 22 Apr. 1705, SANM II:110.
7. Juan de Ulibarrí, Muster, Santa Cruz, 27 Apr. 1705, SANM II:110.
8. Reeve, "Navaho-Spanish Wars," 216. Flagler, "Defensive Policy," 94.
9. Cabildo of Santa Fe, Certification, Santa Fe, 13 Oct. 1705, AGN Provincias Internas, 36:5. Copies in AGI Guadalajara, 116, and BNM 5:10. Reeve, "Navaho-Spanish Wars," 222.
10. Oakah L. Jones, *Pueblo Warriors and Spanish Conquest* (Norman, 1966), 65.
11. Flagler, "Defensive Policy," 93–94.
12. Jones, *Pueblo Warriors,* 71–72.
13. Elizabeth A. H. John, *Storms Brewed in Other Men's Worlds: The Confrontation of Indians, Spanish, and French in the Southwest, 1540–1795* (Lincoln, 1981), 227.
14. Roque Madrid, Receipt, n.p., 23 Aug. 1705, AGN Provincias Internas, 36:5. There is a copy in BNM 5:6. Reeve, "Navaho-Spanish Wars," 216.
15. The number of horses also provides useful information for determining the size of the fighting force. For his 1719 campaign against the Comanches, Antonio Valverde Cosío commanded six hundred men, including presidial troops, militiamen, and Indian allies. The militiamen and Indians in this force had more than 850 horses at their disposal, not counting the mounts of the regular soldiers. Jones, *Pueblo Warriors,* 28, 94–95, 98–99, 103, 117.
16. Frederick Webb Hodge, "The Early Navaho and Apache," *American Anthropologist* 8 (o.s.)(1895): 223–40. Charles Amsden, "Navaho Origins," NMHR 7 (1932): 193–209. Donald E. Worcester, "The Navaho During the Spanish Regime in New Mexico," NMHR 26 (1951): 101–118. Frank D. Reeve, "Early Navaho Geography," NMHR 31 (1956): 290–309. Frank D. Reeve, "Seventeenth Century Navaho-Spanish Relations," NMHR 32 (1957): 36–52. David R. Wilcox, "The Entry of Athapaskans into the American Southwest: The Problem Today," in *The Protohistoric Period in the North American Southwest, AD 1450–1700,* ed. David R. Wilcox and W. Bruce Masse, Arizona State University Anthropological Research Papers, 24 (Tempe, 1981), 213–56. David M. Brugge, "Navajo Prehistory and History to 1850," in *Southwest,* vol. 10 of *Handbook of North American Indians* (Washington, D.C., 1983), 489–501. Frank E. Wozniak, "The Location of the Navajo Homeland in the Seventeenth Century: An Appraisal of the Spanish Colonial

Records," in *Current Research on the Late Prehistory and Early History of New Mexico,* ed. Bradley J. Vierra (Albuquerque, 1992), 327–36.

17. W. W. Hill, "Some Navaho Culture Changes During Two Centuries (with a Translation of the Early Eighteenth Century Rabal Manuscript)," in *Essays in Historical Anthropology of North America,* Smithsonian Miscellaneous Collections, vol. 100 (Washington, D.C., 1940), 395–415. Reeve, "Seventeenth Century," 46–50. Jack D. Forbes, *Apache, Navaho, and Spaniard* (Norman, 1960), 147–50, 173–76. David M. Brugge, "Early 18th-Century Spanish-Apachean Relations," in *Collected Papers in Honor of Bertha Pauline Dutton,* ed. Albert H. Schroeder (Albuquerque, 1979), 106–8. David M. Brugge, "Eighteenth-Century Fugitives from New Mexico among the Navajos," in *Papers from the Third, Fourth, and Sixth Navajo Studies Conferences,* ed. June-el Piper (Window Rock, 1993), 279–83.

18. In March 1744, fray Carlos Delgado and fray José Yrigoyen traveled to Navajo country to minister to the Indians. The following April, Fathers Delgado and Yrigoyen and fray Pedro Ignacio del Pino went to visit the Navajos. By June, now in the company of fray Miguel Menchero, the *procurador general* of the New Mexico missions, Fathers Delgado, Yrigoyen, and del Pino were back among the Navajos. Franciscan plans to build four missions in Navajo country were delayed by unrest in the colony, however, and the site for the first mission, Cebolleta, was not selected until late in 1748. Fray Juan Bermejo was assigned there. Soon another mission was underway at Encinal, in the hands of fray Juan Sanz de Lezaún. Almost from the outset, it was clear that the Navajos were reluctant to settle in pueblos under the direction of a priest. By mid-April 1750, the Indians at Cebolleta and Encinal had driven off the resident priests, and the missionization effort among the Navajo was abandoned. Frank D. Reeve, "The Navaho-Spanish Peace: 1720's–1770's," NMHR 34 (1959): 12–27. Frank McNitt, *Navajo Wars,* 27–28.

19. John P. Wilson and A. H. Warren, "LA 2298, The Earliest Pueblito?" *Awanyu* 2:1 (1974):19–23. J. Manuel Espinosa, *The Pueblo Indian Revolt of 1696 and the Franciscan Missions in New Mexico* (Norman, 1988). Patrick Hogan, "Navajo-Pueblo Interaction during the Gobernador Phase: A Reassessment of the Evidence," in *Rethinking Navajo Pueblitos,* Cultural Resources Series, 8, contribs. Michael P. Marshall and Patrick Hogan (Farmington, 1991).

20. David M. Brugge, "Navajo History," *The Navajo Times,* 9 Sept. 1965, 8B–9B, 23B; "Origin of the Ma'iidesgizhnii Clan," *The Navajo*

Times, 9 June 1966, 9; "Origin of the Nakaidene's and Toyahedliinii Clans," *The Navajo Times,* 8 Sept. 1966, 29B. Brugge, "Early 18th-Century," 120.

21. Wilcox, "Entry," 217. David M. Brugge, "Discussion of Athabaskan Research," in *Current Research on the Late Prehistory and Early History of New Mexico,* ed. Bradley J. Vierra (Albuquerque, 1992), 337.

22. Alfred V. Kidder, "Ruins of the Historic Period in the Upper San Juan Valley, New Mexico," *American Anthropologist* 22 (1920): 322–29.

23. Roy L. Carlson, *Eighteenth Century Navajo Fortresses of the Gobernador District,* University of Colorado Series in Anthropology, 10 (Boulder, 1965). Wilson and Warren, "LA 2298." Margaret A. Powers and Byron P. Johnson, *Defensive Sites of Dinetah,* Cultural Resources Series, 2 (Albuquerque, 1987). Michael P. Marshall, "The Pueblito as a Site Complex: Archeological Investigations in the Dinetah District," in *Rethinking Navajo Pueblitos,* Cultural Resources Series, 8, contribs. Michael P. Marshall and Patrick Hogan (Farmington, 1991).

24. Hill, "Some Navaho Culture Changes."

25. See conclusion, this volume; also Frank D. Reeve, "Navaho-Spanish Wars, 1680–1720," NMHR 33 (1958):205–31.

26. Albert H. Schroeder, "A Brief History of the Southern Utes," *Southwestern Lore* 30 (1965):53–78. J. Lee Correll, "Events in Navajo History No. 18: Navajo-Ute Relations Prior to the 1870s and Naahoondzho 'The Fearing Time'," *The Navajo Times,* 26 Jan. 1967, 10–11. LouAnn Jacobson, Stephen Fosberg, and Robert Bewley, "Navajo Defensive Systems in the Eighteenth Century," in *Cultural Diversity and Adaptation: The Archaic, Anasazi, and Navajo Occupation of the Upper San Juan Basin,* Cultural Resources Series, 9, ed. Lori Stephens Reed and Paul F. Reed (Santa Fe, 1992), 110.

27. James J. Hester, *Early Navajo Migrations and Acculturation in the Southwest,* Museum of New Mexico Papers in Anthropology, 6 (Santa Fe, 1962), 62–63, 80, 82. Bryant Bannister, *Tree-Ring Dating of the Archeological Sites in the Chaco Canyon Region, New Mexico,* Southwestern Monuments Association Technical Series, 6 (Pt. 2) (Globe, 1965), 155–57. Bryant Bannister, William J. Robinson, and Richard L. Warren, *Tree-Ring Dates from New Mexico A, G–H. Shiprock–Zuni–Mt. Taylor Area* (Tucson, 1970). William J. Robinson, Bruce G. Harrill, and Richard L. Warren, *Tree-Ring Dates from New*

Mexico B. Chaco-Gobernador Area (Tucson, 1974). Morris E. Opler, "The Apachean Culture Pattern and Its Origins," in *Handbook* 10:381. Robert W. Young, "Apachean Languages," in *Handbook* 10:393.
28. George P. Hammond and Agapito Rey, *Don Juan de Oñate, Colonizer of New Mexico, 1595–1628*, vol. 2 (Albuquerque, 1953).
29. Alfred E. Dittert, Jr., "Salvage Archaeology and the Navajo Project: A Progress Report," *El Palacio* 65 (1958): 68. Hester, *Early Navajo*, 62–63.
30. Michael P. Marshall, *The Excavation of the Cortez CO_2 Pipeline Project Sites, 1982–1983*, (Albuquerque, 1985). Joseph C. Winter and Patrick Hogan, "The Dinetah Phase of Northwestern New Mexico: Settlement and Subsistence," in *Current Research on the Late Prehistory and Early History of New Mexico*, ed. Bradley J. Vierra (Albuquerque, 1992), 303–6.
31. Regge N. Wiseman, *An Archaeological Clearance Investigation and Impact Statement of Two Southern Union Gas Company Cathodic Protection Lines South of Gobernador, New Mexico*, Museum of New Mexico Laboratory of Anthropology Note No. 122 (Santa Fe, 1975).
32. Lori Stephens Reed and Paul F. Reed, "The Protohistoric Navajo: Implications of Interaction, Exchange, and Alliance Formation with the Eastern and Western Pueblos," in *Cultural Diversity and Adaptation: The Archaic, Anasazi, and Navajo Occupation of the Upper San Juan Basin*, Cultural Resources Series, 9, ed. Lori Stephens Reed and Paul F. Reed (Santa Fe, 1992), 91–104.
33. Alan D. Reed and Jonathan C. Horn, "Early Navajo Occupation of the American Southwest: Reexamination of the Dinetah Phase," *Kiva* 55 (1990): 293.
34. Alan C. Reed et al., *Excavations at Three Early Navajo Sites in the La Plata Valley*, Division of Conservation Archaeology Studies in Archaeology, 7 (Farmington, 1988). Patrick Hogan, "Dinetah: A Reevaluation of Pre-Revolt Navajo Occupation in Northwest New Mexico," *Journal of Anthropological Research* 45 (1989). A. Reed and Horn, "Early Navajo." Patricia M. Hancock, "Evidence of the Dinetah Phase in the La Plata River Valley, San Juan County, New Mexico," in *Current Research on the Late Prehistory and Early History of New Mexico*, ed. Bradley J. Vierra (Albuquerque, 1992), 287–97. Winter and Hogan, "The Dinetah Phase."
35. Gary M. Brown, "Old Wood and Early Navajos: A Chronometric Analysis of the Dinetah Phase," paper presented at Fifth Annual

Navajo Studies Conference (Shiprock, 1990). Gary M. Brown and Patricia M. Hancock, "The Dinetah Phase in the La Plata Valley," in *Cultural Diversity and Adaptation: The Archaic, Anasazi, and Navajo Occupation of the Upper San Juan Basin,* Cultural Resources Series, 9, ed. Lori Stephens Reed and Paul F. Reed (Santa Fe, 1992), 88.

36. Hodge, "The Early Navaho." Amsden, "Navaho Origins," 196–97.
37. Wilcox, "The Entry of Athapaskans," 215–17. Richard J. Perry, "The Apachean Transition from the Subarctic to the Southwest," *Plains Anthropologist* 25(90)(1980): 279–96. Richard J. Perry, *Western Apache Heritage: People of the Mountain Corridor* (Austin, 1991).
38. Reed and Reed, "The Protohistoric Navajo," 97–102. Gary M. Brown, et al., *Archaeological Investigations at Grassy Canyon: A Gobernador Phase Navajo Habitation in the Navajo Reservoir District,* Mariah Associates, Inc., Technical Report No. 535 (Albuquerque, 1992).
39. Amsden, "Navaho Origins," 199–200. Forbes, *Apache,* 115. Alicia Ronstadt Milich, trans., *Relaciones by Zárate Salmerón* (Albuquerque, 1966), 94, 118
40. James H. Gunnerson, "Plateau Shoshonean Prehistory: A Suggested Reconstruction," *American Antiquity* 28 (1962): 41–45. Gary A. Wright, "The Shoshonean Migration Problem," *Plains Anthropologist* 23(80) (1978): 113–37.

Roque Madrid's 1705 Campaign Journal

Note: Our goal in translating Roque Madrid's campaign journal is to provide an accurate, idiomatic English rendering of the original Spanish. To assist the reader, we have supplied paragraphing, punctuation, and specific nouns to clarify confusing antecedents. Proper nouns are retained in Spanish.

1. Madrid's selection of Nuestra Señora de Covadonga, or Our Lady of Covadonga, harkened back to one of the most celebrated places in the history of the Spanish Reconquest. At Covadonga, in the year 718, a Visigothic noble, Pelagius (popularly known as don Pelayo) defeated the troops of the Moorish governor and launched the centuries-long struggle to win back the Iberian Peninsula for Christendom. Since the middle of the eighth century, the Virgin of Covadonga has been venerated; her festival is celebrated on 6 September. *Enciclopedia universal ilustrada europeo-americana,* 15:1409. Roger Collins, *Early Medieval Spain: Unity in Diversity, 400–1000* (New York, 1983), 184, 228.

2. There were at least three campaigns to Navajo country in the period 1675–78 to which Madrid might have been referring, the last one, in October 1678, being the most likely. Although these documents consistently refer to Apaches, that they were Navajos is clear from the geographical context.

On 24 September 1675, Gov. Juan Francisco Treviño commissioned Maestre de campo Juan Domínguez de Mendoza to lead forty harquebusiers and three hundred Indian auxiliaries armed with bows and arrows on a punitive expedition against the Navajos. They were to assemble at Zia on the last day of the month and strike out for the Navajo and Casa Fuerte ranges.

The results included killing fifteen of the enemy; the rescue from captivity of six Christian Indians and one girl, who was the daughter of a Hispanic citizen; the capture of thirty-five Navajos; and the burning of large amounts of maize and other provisions. According to a certification issued in August of 1677, the expedition was in retaliation for the deaths of colonists and raids on churches and herds by Navajos.

Domínguez de Mendoza received another commission to command troops on a campaign into Navajo country on 12 July 1678 from Gov. Antonio de Otermín. Killings, livestock thefts, the destruction of churches and carrying off of sacred vessels, and even the death of ministers and soldiers had led Otermín to conclude that the Indians were bent on the destruction of the colony. Following a daylight raid against Santa Fe, which demonstrated that even the capital was vulnerable, the governor ordered a retaliatory expedition.

Domínguez de Mendoza was to lead fifty mounted harquebusiers and four hundred Indian auxiliaries west from Zia after passing muster there. Their aim was to destroy the fields in the jurisdiction of Casa Fuerte, Navajo, Río Grande, and anywhere else the enemy might be found. Above all they were to try to recover the chalice, patens, and sacred vestments. In addition Domínguez de Mendoza was charged with rescuing three Hispanic women and the Christian Indians who had been carried off from various pueblos.

In the Piedra Lumbre range, he was to punish the enemy who attacked the jurisdiction of La Cañada and recover the bones of Capts. Alonso Fernández and Juan de Herrera, victims of the Navajo.

A little over a month later, Governor Otermín certified the success of Domínguez de Mendoza's expedition. The recent campaign produced fifty male captives along with their wives and children. Two captive women, presumably the Hispanics sought after, were rescued. The Indians' fields were destroyed, and thirteen horses and other goods were taken.

On 28 October 1678, Otermín ordered Domínguez de Mendoza to lead an expedition consisting of the same number of troops and auxiliaries as the one the previous July. As before the motive was retaliation for Navajo depredations, particularly a raid bent on destroying Acoma. The force was to depart Zia and travel to the western ranges of Casa Fuerte, Navajo, and Peñoles, with the aim of destroying their store of provisions for the coming winter.

In a certification of Domínguez de Mendoza's services and in a grant of encomienda issued the following month, Governor Otermín summed up the expedition. More than 2,500 fanegas of maize were burned and an unspecified number of women and children captured. The enemy was routed despite an ambush laid on a mesa top, their houses destroyed, and some Christian captives freed.

While France V. Scholes and Eleanor B. Adams have challenged the authenticity of some of the documents in the Juan Domínguez papers, labeling them forgeries, they did not question the documents cited here. Adams's transcripts with editorial emendations are found among the Scholes papers. University of New Mexico, Center for Southwest Research, Manuscript Collection 360, Box 11, Folder 1d. Antonio de Otermín to Juan Domínguez de Mendoza, Commission, Santa Fe, 28 Oct. 1678; Antonio de Otermín to Juan Domínguez de Mendoza, Instruction, Santa Fe, 28 Oct. 1678; and Antonio de Otermín to Juan Domínguez de Mendoza, Grant of encomienda, Santa Fe, 26 Nov. 1678, BNMad., MS 19258, ff. 129–30, 137–38. Antonio de Otermín to Juan Domínguez de Mendoza, Commission, Santa Fe, 12 July 1678; Antonio de Otermín to Juan Domínguez de Mendoza, Instruction, Santa Fe, 12 July 1678; and Antonio de Otermín, Certification of the services of Juan Domínguez de Mendoza, Santa Fe, 28 Aug. 1678, BNMad., MS 19258, ff. 134–36, 139–41. Juan Francisco Treviño to Juan Domínguez de Mendoza, Commission, Santa Fe, 24 Sept. 1675; and Juan Francisco Treviño, Certification of the services of Juan Domínguez de Mendoza, Santa Fe, 10 Aug. 1677, BNMad., MS 19258, ff. 78–81. Forbes, *Apache,* 173–74. Reeve, "Seventeenth-Century," 49–50. Wozniak, "Location of the Navajo Homeland," 330–31.

3. The birds Madrid identified as partridges, which are Old World fowl, were probably dusky or blue grouse (*Dendragapus obscurus*). The dusky grouse's range is from 7,000 feet to the timber line,

principally in the Sangre de Cristo and Jemez mountains in north-central New Mexico. It also lives in the zone covered by gambel oak (*Quercus gambelii*) between El Rito Creek and the Chama River drainages north to the San Juan Mountains in Colorado. While a number of other upland game birds generally fit the description in the document, factors such as the season, altitude, range, and size militate against them. J. Stokley Ligon, *New Mexico Birds and Where to Find Them* (Albuquerque, 1961), 84–86.

4. The choice of the name Sierra de las Grullas was especially apt. Madrid's expedition traversed an area that was and still is within the flyway of the greater sandhill (*Grus canadensis tabida*) and whooping (*Grus americana*) cranes. Nevertheless he is one of the few Spaniards in New Mexico to remark on these magnificent birds. Dale Stahlecker and Martin Frentzel, *Seasons of the Crane* (Albuquerque, 1986), 31–32, 53–54.

5. *Escopeta* is used in the general sense of firearm. At this time, *escopeta, harquebus,* and *fusil* were synonymous terms referring to a flintlock firearm, in contrast to the *mosquete,* which was a matchlock. Fray Francisco de Ayeta, commenting on the request of the Santa Fe cabildo for supplies for the refugees from the Pueblo Revolt, specified that they needed flintlock harquebuses with six thousand additional flints (1 January 1681). In the early sixteenth century, the term *harquebus* referred to the firearm supplied with a matchlock, but by the turn of the century it had begun to be applied to the one with a wheellock. During the early eighteenth century in New Spain, the harquebus could be fitted with a flintlock. Harold L. Peterson, *Arms and Armor in Colonial America, 1526–1783* (New York, 1956), 12–13. Charles Wilson Hackett, ed., and Charmion Clair Shelby, trans., *Revolt of the Pueblo Indians of New Mexico and Otermín's Attempted Reconquest, 1680–1682* (Albuquerque, 1942), 1:238.

6. Throughout the reconquest of New Mexico, in which Madrid participated, Mary was invoked in her role as intercessor. In Catholic theology, she is considered the mediatrix of all graces. Mary's mediation serves to bring about the reconciliation of God and humankind through her son. Through her intercession in heaven, she obtains and is the dispensatrix of the grace that God chooses to bestow on humankind, of whom she is the spiritual mother.

Nuestra Señora de la Conquista, or Our Lady of the Conquest, is also known as Our Lady of the Rosary or Our Lady of Remedies. Our Lady of Remedies was Diego de Vargas's special protector.

Throughout the 1692 expedition, the alferez of the company carried a banner that bore on one side an image of Our Lady of Remedies. Vargas requested her mediation to bring about the return of the Pueblo Indians to the faith. According to Vargas, Our Lady of Remedies made a miraculous intercession, though not an apparition, at Awatovi on 19 November 1692. After successfully carrying out the largely ceremonial reconquest, Vargas referred to her as Our Lady of the Conquest. This modification of nomenclature follows that of Hernán Cortés, who carried an image of Our Lady of Remedies and referred to her as Our Lady of the Conquest as well. Some confusion in this matter results from the fact that the Our Lady of the Conquest venerated in Santa Fe to the present day is actually an image of Our Lady of the Rosary. The cult of Our Lady of Remedies is confined to Spain and Latin America. Notable images can be found in Bolivia, Colombia, Guatemala, Mexico, and Peru. In addition the official name of the Santa Fe presidio was the Presidio of the Exaltation of the Cross and Our Lady of Remedies. Proceedings in the matter of the soldiers of the presidio of Santa Fe *v.* Francisco Cuervo y Valdés, Santa Fe, 16 Dec. 1710, AGN Cárceles y presidios, 18:1–4. Rubén Vargas Ugarte, *Historia del culto de María en Iberoamérica y de sus imágenes y santuarios más celebrados* (Madrid, 1956), 1:300, 370–71, 393, 397; 2:158, 285. J. Manuel Espinosa, "The Virgin of the Reconquest of New Mexico," *Mid-America* 18 (Apr. 1936): 79. Juniper B. Carol, ed., *Mariology* (Milwaukee, 1961), 1:32–44. José M. Bover, *María mediadora universal o soteriología mariana estudiada a la luz de principios mariológicos* (Madrid, 1946), 34–49. NCE, 9:359. *The Liturgy of the Hours According to the Roman Rite* (New York, 1975), 1368.

7. In New Spain, *genízaro* was sometimes used in the sense of mestizo or a person of mixed Indian and non-Indian blood. In eighteenth- and nineteenth-century New Mexico, it became a specialized ethnic term for a group derived from detribalized Indians, mostly women and children, captured during intertribal raids and ransomed to Spanish households to be used as servants. The offspring of these servants, the actual genízaros, followed local Hispanic custom and usually lost their tribal identity.

Some genízaros, however, referred to themselves and were referred to by their contemporaries as genízaros of a given Indian nation. Two examples, widely separated in time and place in colonial New Mexico, illustrate this point. In late November 1692 at the pueblo of Halona, Diego de Vargas obtained information from an individual described as "a genízaro Zuni." In El Paso seventy-six years later, in making out her will, María Antonia Roybal referred to herself as "a genízara of the Apache nation" and to her husband as "a genízaro of the Kiowa nation." María Antonia Roybal, Will, El Paso, 20 Dec. 1768, Juárez Municipal Archives (second filming), r. 8, bk. 1, 1764, ff. 699–706. John L. Kessell and Rick Hendricks, eds., *By Force of Arms: The Journals of don Diego de Vargas, New Mexico, 1691–93* (Albuquerque, 1992), 606. Robert Archibald, "Acculturation and Assimilation in Colonial New Mexico," NMHR 53 (July 1978): 210–14. Fray Angelico Chavez, "Genízaros," in *Southwest,* vol. 9 of *Handbook of North American Indians* (Washington, D.C., 1983), 198–99.

8. According to a statement given in 1704 by Tomás Girón, the governor of Santa Clara, Tewas who had been taken off by people he referred to as Apaches during the Pueblo Revolt of 1696 had suffered greatly. Pamuje might have been one of these Pueblo refugees who did not remain among the Navajos. Brugge, "Early 18th-Century," 104.

9. This episode is similar in some respects to the greeting that Pedro de Tovar received from the Hopis in the province of Tusayán in the autumn of 1540. As the chronicler Pedro de Castañeda recorded it, Hopis drew a line on the ground with sacred cornmeal. On that occasion, the Spaniards interpreted this as a warning, and a battle soon ensued. On the 1705 campaign, no indication was given as to how the Navajos made the lines and crosses. Madrid read them as an indication that the Navajos did not want the Spaniards to come closer and were ill-prepared to meet them. It is possible that in both instances, the Spaniards misunderstood the symbolism of the message, which could well have been imbued with religious meaning, given the presence of sacred cornmeal and crosses. Herbert E. Bolton, *Coronado: Knight of Pueblos and Plains* (Albuquerque, 1980), 136.

10. Half a pack animal's load, or carga, was divided into two tercios, when the load went into bundles (*fardos*). A carga weighed about 135 kilograms.

11. Pinole (Nahuatl *pinolli* from *piniol-atl*) was meal or flour made from parched maize or other grains and used, when beaten into cold or hot water, as a drink. Sometimes honey, sugar, chocolate, cinnamon, vanilla, or other ingredients were added. The term also refers to the drink itself.

12. The use of night marches was a standard tactic employed by Spanish troops in the Americas. As early as 1599, Bernardo de Vargas Machuca spelled out the advantages of troop movements under cover of darkness. He especially recommended night marches when a province was in revolt. The soldiers were to guard against making noise at all times. Rain storms were held to be particularly helpful, since they dampened the sound and kept the enemy in their homes. Commanders and their men alike were cautioned not to shout out, should they fall and injure themselves.

    In his many years of campaigning in New Mexico with Diego de Vargas, Roque Madrid often had occasion to participate in night marches, which Vargas explained in this way:

    > The enemy is always camped on ridges, mesas, and canyons of very rugged mountains, as these are. It is even necessary to march all night in order to avoid being perceived by the enemy and, on occasion, into the morning, because one cannot measure time by distance when it is over such difficult terrain.

    Kessell and Hendricks, *By Force of Arms,* 58. Bernardo de Vargas Machuca, *Milicia y descripción de las Indias* (1599; reprint, Madrid, 1892) 1:225–36.

13. Spaniards invoked Santiago, or St. James, the patron saint of Spain, when they began a battle. This was referred to as giving the Santiago.

14. According to the terminology usually applied to the various types of Hispanic-held property in eighteenth-century New Mexico, a rancho was one or more households living on a relatively small farm. Nevertheless *rancho* is also commonly used to describe a hut. Used in this latter sense, it would suggest that Madrid's troops encountered simple field houses at the milpas located in the canyons. Marc Simmons, "Settlement Patterns and Village Plans in Colonial New Mexico," in *New Spain's Far Northern Frontier: Essays on Spain in the American West, 1540–1821,* ed. David J. Weber (Albuquerque, 1979), 103–6.

15. By contrast to the ranchos and houses mentioned above, the use of *rancheria* suggests that the Navajos in the uplands were living in a more complex settlement pattern, in multifamily homesites. David M. Brugge, pers. comm., Nov. 1994.

16. North American Indians practiced scalping before European contact. In the Southwest, warrior or scalp societies formed an integral part of Puebloan life. A man became a warrior and a

member of such a society after killing an enemy, taking his scalp, and completing requisite rituals with it. Sometimes the entire scalp was removed with the ears; other times it was taken from the crown of the head. Among the Hopis, dead enemies were scalped only if they had fought bravely. The people greeted returning warriors and began a ritual process by which the scalps were purified and eventually "adopted" into the tribe. Among the Tewas, members of the Women's Scalp Association took enemy scalps from the returning war party and chewed them while cursing the enemy. In some cases at Hopi, the women would take small bits of the remaining flesh from the scalp and feed them to their children to encourage bravery. It was believed that enemy scalps could bring good to the tribe, if handled properly. The war chief was responsible for them; often they would be hung on shields in a kiva or on its walls. In the Puebloan Southwest, scalps were considered bringers of rain and sometimes seeds. Ritual names for scalps often had linguistic associations with words reflecting different forms of moisture, such as mist or rain. It is traditional belief that when it is going to rain, the scalps cry. The war chief, sometimes with the help of the women's branch of the war society, took care of the scalps by ritually washing them and feeding them sacred cornmeal or pollen. James Axtell, "The Unkindest Cut, or Who Invented Scalping," in *The European and the Indian: Essays in the Ethnohistory of Colonial North America* (New York, 1981), 27. Charles H. Lange, *Cochiti: A New Mexico Pueblo, Past and Present* (Austin, 1959), 250. Alexander M. Stephen, *Hopi Journal of Alexander M. Stephen,* ed. Elsie C. Parsons, (New York, 1936), 2:98–99. Edward P. Dozier, *The Pueblo Indians of North America* (New York, 1970), 81. Leslie A. White, *The Acoma Indians: People of the Sky City,* 47th Annual Report of the Bureau of American Ethnology (Washington, D.C., 1932), 99. Pauline Turner Strong, "Santa Ana Pueblo," *Handbook* 9:401. Dennis Tedlock, "Zuni Religion and World View," *Handbook* 9:501. Richard J. Parmentier, "The Pueblo Mythological Triangle: Poseyemu, Montezuma, and Jesus in the Pueblos," *Handbook* 9:610–11.

17. The term *chusma* was used to refer to Indians who were generally considered noncombatants: women, children, and the elderly. Francisco J. Santamaría, *Diccionario de mejicanismos* (Mexico City, 1983), 428.
18. The decision to take his own life rather than face possible execution or imprisonment was probably very different for a Navajo than for a

Spaniard. In the Navajo world view, the way in which one lives one's life on earth does not determine one's situation after death. While by no means a universal belief, some Navajos hold to the view that witches and suicides live separated from everyone else in the afterworld. Some Navajos also jumped to their death to avoid capture following a battle at Beautiful Mountain in 1818. After major defeats, some Pueblo Indians opted for death rather than falling into the hands of their conquerors, such as at Acoma in 1599 and in the aftermath of the battle of Santa Fe in 1693. John L. Kessell, Rick Hendricks, and Meredith D. Dodge, *To the Royal Crown Restored: The Journals of don Diego de Vargas,* 1692–94 (Albuquerque, 1995), 533. McNitt, *Navajo Wars,* 83. Hammond and Rey, *Don Juan de Oñate,* 1:462. Clyde Kluckhohn and Dorothea Leighton, *The Navajo* (Cambridge, Mass., 1960), 232.

19. The text in parenthesis was written later and marked for insertion at this point in the journal.

Spanish Version of the Journal

Note: Sender Collection, 2 and 3, State Records Center and Archives, Santa Fe. A holographic transcription in the hand of Adolphe Eugene Bandelier, with minor emendations by Adolph Bandelier, is found in the Hemenway Expedition Collections, Peabody Museum Library (Rare Book Room, Tozzer Library, Harvard University). There are a few minor transcription errors in the Bandeliers' transcription.

Adolph's comments indicate that the original document formed a part of the New Mexico General Territorial Archive, which was scattered and damaged in 1870–71. In August 1889, the document was in the possession of José Segura of Santa Fe, his father having saved it from destruction. Adolph indicated that he had verified and corrected his father's transcription on 26 August 1889 in Santa Fe.

In the main our transcription adheres to the norms of modern Spanish orthography; such archaic forms that we have retained are noted. We have supplied paragraphing and punctuation. In the case of nouns used as place names, we have also supplied capitalization.

1. Alvarez Castrillón wrote *Tierra* here, but later corrected himself.
2. The Spanish Real Academia de la Lengua did not dictate the disappearance of "ph" for "f" until the fourth edition of its *Diccionario* (1803). We have retained this spelling in the text where it is associated with a place or person. Robert K. Spaulding, *How Spanish Grew* (Berkeley, 1943), 189.

3. We have retained the fossilized form *vide* for *ví* because it is still quite common in Southwestern Spanish.
4. The original has *voracidad* (*borasidad*), or "voracity," but the scribe overwrote the initial letter, which may indicate lexical uncertainty. At any rate, *ferocidad*, translated as "with fury," seems to fit the context better.

THE ROUTE OF THE CAMPAIGN

1. Father Vélez de Escalante obviously consulted a source—no longer available—other than the campaign journal to provide these casualty figures. Vélez de Escalante, Extracto de noticias, BNM 3:1.
2. Kessell and Hendricks, *By Force of Arms*, 447.
3. Eleanor B. Adams and Fray Angelico Chavez, trans. and annot., *The Missions of New Mexico, 1776: A Description by Fray Francisco Atanasio Domínguez with other Contemporary Documents* (Albuquerque, 1956), 92.
4. Robert W. Frazer, "The Battle of Cienguilla," *La Crónica de Nuevo México*, 9 (Santa Fe, 1980): 3–5.
5. T. M. Pearce, *New Mexico Place Names* (Albuquerque, 1965), 169.
6. Frank D. Reeve, "Early Navaho Geography," NMHR 31 (1956): 300–1.
7. Charles Glover, "Classification of Irrigation Water," New Mexico State University Cooperative Extension Service Guide A-110 (1984); also New Mexico State University Soil, Water, and Plant Testing Laboratory, Water Analysis Report, Lab No. 7156 (June 6, 1988).
8. New Mexico Office of Cultural Affairs, Historic Preservation Division, Archeological Records Management System, LA 8948 site files.
9. Dr. William J. Robinson, Laboratory of Tree-Ring Research, pers. comm. to John P. Wilson, 23 Aug. 1973.
10. Wilson and Warren, "LA 2298," 8–26. Powers and Johnson, *Defensive Sites*, 27–28, 125–27. Marshall, "Pueblito as a Site Complex," 89–100. Ronald H. Towner and Jeffrey S. Dean, "LA 2298: The Oldest Pueblito Revisited," *Kiva* 57 (1992): 315–29.
11. Reeve, "Navaho-Spanish Peace," 15.
12. Chas. C. Morrison, "Executive and Descriptive Report of Lieutenant C. C. Morrison, Sixth Cavalry, on the Operations of Party No. 2, Colorado Section, Field-Season of 1875," Appendix E to Appendix JJ, George M. Wheeler, Annual Report, Geographical Surveys West

of the 100th Meridian, in *Annual Report of the Chief of Engineers for 1876* (Washington, D.C., 1876), 359.

Conclusion

1. Fray Juan de Tagle, Letter-patent, Santa Fe, 9 Sept. 1705, AASF, 1705:3.
2. Francisco Cuervo y Valdés, Certification, Santa Fe, 6 Oct. 1705, Huntington Library.
3. Tafoya's statement is somewhat problematic. If he was referring to the September campaign, the Spaniards returned to Navajo country by way of the Sierra de las Grullas, despite having found that way in to be extremely difficult. The distance traveled and the geographical features he describes are remarkably similar to those seen in August 1705, although he fails to mention Los Peñoles and recalls that the expedition returned by way of Cerro de los Pedernales, near Abiquiu. Given the distance between the two points, it seems unlikely that he was confusing Abiquiu with Zia. Nevertheless, it is plausible that he was a participant in the August expedition under Roque Madrid's command. Antonio Tafoya, Statement, Santa Fe, 6 Mar. 1745, Univ. of California, Bancroft Library, New Mexico Originals, microfilm collection, r. 1. Reeve, "Navaho-Spanish Wars," 221–22.
4. The term *jícara,* from the Nahuatl *xicalli,* originally referred to a cup used for drinking chocolate and fashioned from the fruit of a tree of the same name. Over time the term came to be used for any cup, particularly those made from gourds. By 1700 Gov. Pedro Rodríguez Cubero was using the term, in its diminutive form, to describe Apaches (Jicarillas) who made hemispheric baskets. Veronica E. Velarde Tiller, *The Jicarilla Apache Tribe: A History, 1846–1970* (Lincoln, 1983), 5. Santamaría, *Diccionario,* 633–34.
5. Cabildo of Santa Fe, Certification, Santa Fe, 13 Oct. 1705, AGN Provincias Internas, 36:5. Copies in AGI Guadalajara, 116, and BNM 5:10. Reeve, "Navaho-Spanish Wars," 222.
6. Fray Juan de Tagle, Certification, Santa Fe, 17 Oct. 1705, AGN Provincias Internas, 35:6. Copies in AGI Guadalajara, 116 and BNM 5:10.
7. Vélez de Escalante, Extracto de noticias.
8. Francisco Cuervo y Valdés to the king, Santa Fe, 16 Nov. 1705, AGI Guadalajara, 116. Cabildo of Santa Fe, Certification, Santa Fe, 13 Oct. 1705, AGN Provincias Internas, 36:5. Fray Juan de Tagle,

Certification, Santa Fe, 17 Oct. 1705, AGN Provincias Internas, 35:6. Francisco Cuervo y Valdés to the Duque de Alburquerque, Santa Fe, 23 Oct. 1705, AGN Provincias Internas, 36:5. Alfonso Rael de Aguilar, Certification, Santa Fe, 6 Jan. 1707, AGN Provincias Internas, 36:1. See Hogan, "Navajo-Pueblo Interaction," 16–22.

9. Hogan, "Navajo-Pueblo Interaction," 17–19.
10. Blas Martín, Statement, Santa Fe, 27 Feb. 1745, Univ. of California, Bancroft Library, New Mexico Originals, microfilm collection, r. 1.
11. Ernest J. Burrus, S.J., *Kino and Manje: Explorers of Sonora and Arizona* (Rome, 1971), 399, 423, 438, 443.
12. Alfonso Rael de Aguilar, Certification, Santa Fe, 10 Jan. 1706, AGN Provincias Internas, 36:5. There are copies in BNM 5:6 and 5:8. The copy in AGI Guadalajara, 116, is cited in Flagler, "Defensive Policy," 95.
13. Cabildo of Santa Fe, Certification, Santa Fe, 23 Feb. 1706, AGN Provincias Internas, 36:5. There are copies in BNM 5:6 and 5:8. The copy in AGI Guadalajara is cited in Flagler, "Defensive Policy," 97. The AGN document is discussed in Brugge, "Early 18th-Century," 108–10.
14. Francisco Cuervo y Valdés to the Conde de Alburquerque, Santa Fe, 26 Apr. 1706, AGN Provincias Internas, 36:5. There are copies in BNM 5:6 and 5:8. Francisco Cuervo y Valdés to the Duque de Alburquerque, Santa Fe, 23 June 1706, AGN Provincias Internas, 36:5. There are copies in BNM 5:6 and 5:8
15. Reeve expressed doubt that Navajos grew cotton. Reeve, "Navaho-Spanish Wars," 217. Francisco Cuervo y Valdés to the Duque de Alburquerque, Santa Fe, 23 June 1706, AGN Provincias Internas, 36:5. Cuervo y Valdés also provided this information in a letter to the king, cited in Casado Fuente, "Don Francisco Cuerbo y Valdés," 64–65, and in Flagler, "Defensive Policy," 96. Vélez de Escalante, Extracto de noticias. Curtis F. Schaafsma, "A Review of the Documentary Evidence for a Seventeenth-Century Navajo Occupation in the Chama Valley," in *Current Research on the Late Prehistory and Early History of New Mexico,* ed. Bradley J. Vierra (Albuquerque, 1992), 320–21. Charles Wilson Hackett, ed., *Historical Documents Relating to New Mexico, Nueva Vizcaya, and Approaches Thereto, to 1773* (Washington, D.C., 1937), 3:381–83.
16. Cabildo of Santa Fe, Certification, Santa Fe, 23 Feb. 1706, AGN Provincias Internas, 36:5. The copy in AGI Guadalajara 116 is cited in Casado Fuente, "Don Francisco Cuerbo y Valdés," 68 and in Flagler, "Defensive Policy," 97.

17. Vélez de Escalante, Extracto de noticias.
18. Francisco Cuervo y Valdés, Service record, [Mexico City, 1712], AGI Guadalajara, 116.
19. Brugge, "Early 18th Century Spanish-Apachean Relations," 113–19. Flagler, "Defensive Policy," 100–101. Edward K. Flagler, "Governor José Chacón, Marqués de la Peñuela: An Andalusian Nobleman on the New Mexico Frontier," NMHR 65 (Oct. 1990): 473.
20. The Marqués de la Peñuela, Order, Santa Fe, 21 Feb. 1709, SANM II:154. Reeve, "Navaho-Spanish Wars," 225. Flagler, "Governor José Chacón," 473.
21. Vélez de Escalante, Extracto de noticias. Reeve, "Navaho-Spanish Wars," 225. Flagler, "Governor José Chacón," 473.
22. The Marqués de la Peñuela, Order, Santa Fe, 8 Dec. 1709, SANM II:157. Reeve, "Navaho-Spanish Wars," 225–26.
23. Juan Páez Hurtado, Certification, Santa Fe, 31 Aug. 1713, Huntington Library.
24. The Marqués de la Peñuela, Order, Santa Fe, 8 Dec. 1709, SANM II:157. Flagler, "Governor José Chacón," 474.
25. Vélez de Escalante, Extracto de noticias. Reeve, "Navaho-Spanish Wars," 227.
26. It would seem that the torreones referred to may have been Navajo pueblito sites. Vélez de Escalante, Extracto de noticias. Reeve, "Navaho-Spanish Wars," 228.
27. Antonio de Ulibarrí, Statement, Santa Fe, 4 Mar. 1745, Univ. of California, Bancroft Library, New Mexico Originals, microfilm collection, r. 1. Reeve, "Navaho-Spanish Wars," 229.

Biographical Sketches

1. AASF, Diligencia matrimonial (DM), 1707:6, 1715:7.
2. Since they had the same rather uncommon combination of surnames and both lived in Sonora at one time, it seems probable that Antonio was a relative (perhaps the son) of Capt. Pedro Alvarez Castrillón. Pedro was alcalde mayor of Sonora during the early 1670s. Luis Navarro García, *Sonora y Sinaloa en el siglo xvii* (Seville, 1967), 66. Oakah L. Jones, Jr., *Nueva Vizcaya: Heartland of the Spanish Frontier* (Albuquerque, 1988), 108.
3. AASF, DM, 1707:6.
4. José Chacón Medina Salazar y Villaseñor, Report, Santa Fe, 26 Jan. 1710, AGN Provincias Internas, 36.

5. Ignacio Flores Mogollón, Junta of war, Santa Fe, 5–25 July 1714, SANM II:207.
6. Baltasar Romero to Alejo Gutiérrez, Conveyance of property, Santa Fe, 11 Mar. 1715, SANM I:307.
7. Antonio Fuentes de Sierra, Antonio Alvarez Castrillón, and Juan José González Castrillón, Founding of a capellania, Zacatecas, 7 Aug. 1718, Archivos Históricos del Arzobispado de Durango, r. 15, ff. 440–47.
8. Aguascalientes, Baptisms, LDS:0017062.
9. Information courtesy of Jaime Holcomb of Cabo San Lucas, Baja California Sur, Mexico.
10. Fray Angelico Chavez, O.F.M., The *Origins of New Mexico Families in the Spanish Colonial Period in Two Parts: The Seventeenth (1598–1693), and the Eighteenth (1693–1821) Centuries* (Santa Fe, 1975), 133.
11. Clevy Lloyd Strout, "The Resettlement of Santa Fe, 1695: The Newly Found Muster Roll," NMHR 53 (July 1978): 267.
12. Cristóbal de Arellano, Denunciation, Santa Fe, 27 Nov. 1697, SANM II:71A
13. Pay list for the Santa Fe presidio, Santa Fe, 23 Aug. 1697, AGN Historia, 37:1.
14. Deposition of Cristóbal de Arellano, Santa Fe, 13 Feb. 1700 and Denunciation of Miguel Tenorio de Alba, Santa Fe, 15 Nov. 1698, AGN Vínculos, 14.
15. Bartolomé Lobato, Petition, Santa Fe, 16 Dec. 1703, SANM I:1384.
16. Report of goods that Juan Páez Hurtado gave to Francisco Cuervo y Valdés, Santa Fe, 13 Sept. 1707, AGN Vínculos, 125.
17. Félix Martínez, Proceedings and campaign journal, Santa Fe and Hopi country, 10 May–20 Nov. 1716, SANM II:250. Ralph E. Twitchell's annotated translation, as edited by Bloom, is in Lansing B. Bloom, "A Campaign against the Moqui Pueblos under Governor Phelix Martínez, 1716," NMHR 6 (Apr. 1931): 158–227.
18. Antonio Holguín and Micaela de Moraga, DM, Socorro, 11 Aug. 1707, Catholic Archives of Texas. Fray Angelico Chavez, *Archives of the Archdiocese of Santa Fe, 1678–1900* (Washington, D.C., 1957), 9, 22, 245. Adams and Chavez, *Missions,* 259–60, 264, 329, 334.
19. Criminal case against Gerónimo Dirucaca, Picuris and Santa Fe, 8 May–4 June 1713, SANM II:192. Charles, R. Cutter, *The Protector de*

Indios in Colonial New Mexico, 1659–1821 (Albuquerque, 1986), 54–55.
20. Chavez, *Origins,* 169–70.
21. AASF, DM, 1682:5.
22. Thomas H. Naylor and Charles W. Polzer, comps. and eds., *The Presidio and Militia on the Northern Frontier of New Spain: A Documentary History, 1500–1700* (Tucson, 1986), 1:519.
23. Ernest J. Burrus, S.J., "A Tragic Interlude in the Reconquest of New Mexico," *Manuscripta* 29 (Nov. 1985): 164.
24. Domingo Jironza Petrís de Cruzate, Muster, El Paso, 18 Apr. 1686, BYU. Pedro Reneros de Posada, Muster, El Paso, 17 Apr. 1687, BYU.
25. AASF, DM, 1690:4, 6.
26. Kessell and Hendricks, *By Force of Arms,* 525.
27. AASF, 1705:12.
28. AASF, DM, 1714:4.
29. Ignacio Flores Mogollón, Junta of war, Santa Fe, 9–12 Aug. 1714, SANM II:209. Joseph Domínguez, Opinion, Santa Fe, 5 July 1719, SANM II:309.
30. Félix Martínez, Proceedings and campaign journal, Santa Fe and Hopi country, 10 May–20 Nov. 1716, SANM II:250.
31. Alfred Barnaby Thomas, ed. and trans., *After Coronado: Spanish Exploration Northeast of New Mexico, 1696–1727* (Norman, 1935), 186.
32. AASF, DM, 1727:12.
33. Chavez, *Origins,* 185.
34. Diego de Vertia to Martín García, Land sale, Santa Fe, 6 Feb. 1702, SANM I:290.
35. The Marqués de la Peñuela, Order, Santa Fe, 10 Nov. 1710, SANM II:161.
36. Hackett and Shelby, *Revolt,* 1:148, 150, 2:72, 121, 140, 185, 196. Burrus, "Tragic Interlude," 156, 159.
37. Juan Griego and Juliana Sáis to Diego Arias de Quiros, Land sale, Santa Fe, 21 June 1718, SANM I:716.
38. AASF, DM, 1699:15.
39. AASF, DM, 1716:26
40. Chavez, *Origins,* 192.
41. Diego de Vargas to the Conde de Galve, Letter of transmittal, Santa

Fe, 31 July 1696, AGI Guadalajara, 141:9. Espinosa, *Pueblo Revolt,* 275.
42. Diego de Vargas, Campaign journal, 6 Oct. 1694, San Juan, AGI Guadalajara 140:9. Espinosa, *Pueblo Revolt,* 104.
43. Chavez, *Origins,* 194.
44. Burrus, "Tragic Interlude," 160.
45. Libro de cuentas de los avios y socorros que se les va dando a los cien presidiales de la villa de Santa Fe a cuenta de sueldos cuyos pagamentos hace el capitán don Félix Martínez en virtud de poder de dichos presidiales, Santa Fe, 1712, AGN Civil, 1712.
46. AASF, DM, 1699:2. María Gutiérrez to Alejo Gutiérrez, Donation of land, 7 Aug. 1712, and Alejo Gutiérrez to Antonio López, Conveyance of property, Santa Fe 13 June 1715, SANM I:434
47. Soldiers of the presidio of Santa Fe, Certification, Santa Fe, 15 July 1713, SANM II:192A.
48. Chavez, *Origins,* 194.
49. AASF, DM, 1690:4.
50. AASF, DM, 1709:7.
51. El Paso presidial soldiers to Antonio Valverde Cosío, Power of attorney, El Paso, 19 Apr. 1702, ZCCL, Box 43, Folder 7.
52. Juan Roque Gutiérrez, Opinion, Santa Fe, 16 Apr. 1705, SANM II:110.
53. Francisco Cuervo y Valdés, Muster, Santa Fe, 20 Apr. 1705, and Juan de Ulibarrí, Muster, Bernalillo, 22 Apr. 1705, SANM II:110.
54. Francisco Cuervo y Valdés to Juan Roque Gutiérrez, Letter, Santa Fe, 9 May 1706.
55. Vélez de Escalante, Extracto de noticias, BNM 3:1.
56. Francisco Cuervo y Valdés to Bartolomé Sánchez, Land grant, Santa Fe, 27 July 1707, SANM I:824.
57. Report of goods that Juan Páez Hurtado gave to Francisco Cuervo y Valdés, Santa Fe, 13 Sept. 1707, AGN Vínculos, 125.
58. AASF, DM, 1709:7.
59. Domingo Jironza Petrís de Cruzate, Certification, El Paso, 29 Mar. 1690, ZCCL.
60. AASF, DM 1690:1, 6.
61. AASF, DM, 1709:14, 21–22; 1716:28.
62. Chavez, *Origins,* 196

63. El Paso presidial soldiers to Antonio Valverde Cosío, Power of attorney, El Paso, 19 Apr. 1702, ZCCL.
64. Miguel de Herrera, Opinion, Santa Fe, 16 Apr. 1705, SANM II:110.
65. The Marqués de la Peñuela, Certification, Santa Fe, 16 Dec. 1710, AGN Cárceles y Presidios, 18.
66. Libro de cuentas, Santa Fe, 1712, AGN Civil, 1712. Chavez, *Origins*, 196.
67. Chavez, *Origins*, 244–45.
68. Diego de Vargas, Certification, El Paso, 19 Apr. 1692, ZCCL.
69. Diego de Vargas, Campaign journal, 26 Mar.–31 May 1694, SANM II:55D.
70. Francisco Cuervo y Valdés to Juan Roque Gutiérrez, Letter, Santa Fe, 9 May 1706, SANM II:123.BNM 3:1.
71. Reeve, "Navaho-Spanish Wars," 226.
72. Jones, *Pueblo Warriors*, 88–89.
73. Antonio Holguín and Micaela de Moraga, DM, Socorro, 11 Aug. 1707, Catholic Archives of Texas.
74. Félix Martínez, Proceedings and campaign journal, Santa Fe and Hopi country, 10 May–20 Nov. 1716, SANM II:250.
75. Tomás López to the Marqués de Valero, Santa Fe, 20 July 1717, AGN Cárceles y presidios, 18.
76. Cristóbal de la Serna, Declaration, Mexico City, 24 Sept. 1717, AGN Cárceles y presidios, 18.
77. Thomas, *After Coronado*, 107.
78. Thomas, *After Coronado*, 186. Tomás Holguín, Opinion, 2 June 1720, Santa Fe, AGN Historia, 299. Antonio Valverde Cosío, Junta of war, Santa Fe, 27 May–3 June 1720, SANM II:308.
79. Thomas, *After Coronado*, 184.
80. Thomas, *After Coronado*, 223, 233.
81. Fray Francisco Jiménez, Certification, San Lorenzo de los Picurís, 31 Aug. 1706, AGN Provincias Internas, 36. Francisco Antonio de la Rosa Figueroa, Becerro general menológico y cronológico de todos los religiosos que de las tres parcialidades conviene a saber padres de España, hijos de provincia y criollos ha habido en esta Santa Provincia del Santo Evangelio desde su fundación hasta el presente año de 1764. Newberry Library, Chicago, Ayer Collection.
82. AASF, DM, 1715:10.

83. Diego de Vargas, Campaign journal, Roque Madrid's abandoned hacienda, 15 Dec. 1693, Ritch Collection, 25. Translated in Kessell, Hendricks, and Dodge, *To the Royal Crown Restored,* 467–48.
84. Hackett and Shelby, *Revolt,* 1:119.
85. Hackett and Shelby, *Revolt,* 1:142.
86. Hackett and Shelby, *Revolt,* 2:122.
87. Hackett and Shelby, *Revolt,* 2: 282, 283–84, 286–87, 325–26, 350, 391.
88. Domingo Jironza Petrís de Cruzate, Certification, El Paso, 17 Apr. 1684, ZCCL.
89. Burrus, "Tragic Interlude," 164.
90. Naylor and Polzer, *Presidio,* 1:506–9, 540–42. Kessell and Hendricks, *By Force of Arms,* 23.
91. Domingo Jironza Petrís de Cruzate, Muster, El Paso, 18 Apr. 1686, BYU. Pedro Reneros de Posada, Muster, El Paso, 17 Apr. 1687, BYU.
92. Kessell and Hendricks, *By Force of Arms,* 360, 362–63. J. Manuel Espinosa, *Crusaders of the Río Grande: The Story of Don Diego de Vargas and the Reconquest and Refounding of New Mexico* (Salisbury, N.C., 1977), 50, 53.
93. Espinosa, *Crusaders,* 130.
94. Diego de Vargas to Roque Madrid, Land grant, El Paso, 18 Sept. 1693, SANM I:476.
95. Espinosa, *Crusaders,* 170, 177, 178, 234, 278, 284.
96. Diego de Vargas, Campaign journal, Cochiti Pueblo, 22 Nov. 1693; and Diego de Vargas, Campaign journal, Jemez Pueblo, 25 Nov. 1693, Ritch Collection, 25. Translated in Kessell, Hendricks, and Dodge, *To the Royal Crown Restored,* 425, 437.
97. Espinosa, *Crusaders,* 179–80.
98. Espinosa, *Crusaders,* 245–46, 286.
99. Espinosa, *Crusaders,* 316.
100. Pedro Rodríguez Cubero, Certification, [Santa Fe], 19 Apr. 1700, ZCCL.
101. Edward K. Flagler, "Governor José Chacón, Marqués de la Peñuela: An Andalusian Nobleman on the New Mexico Frontier," NMHR 65 (Oct. 1990): 468.
102. Roque Madrid and Silvestre Pacheco, Compromise, Santa Fe, 2 Dec. 1708, SANM I:488. Roque Madrid, Petition for revalidation of a land grant, Santa Fe, 13 Nov. 1708, SANM I:485. Roque Madrid, Land claim, Santa Fe, 27 Nov. 1708, SANM I:486.

103. The Marqués de la Penuela, Order, Santa Fe, 8 Dec. 1709, SANM II:157. The Marqués de la Penuela, Order, Santa Fe, 21 Feb. 1709, SANM II:154.
104. Roque Madrid, Distribution of tools, Santa Cruz, 3 Jan. 1712, SANM II:169.
105. Roque Madrid, et. al., Petition, Santa Fe, 29 Mar. 1712, SANM I:1020.
106. Presidial company, Santa Fe, 16 May 1713, SANM II:205A.
107. Roque Madrid, Opinion, Santa Fe, 6 July 1714, SANM II, 206. Reeve, "Navaho-Spanish Wars," 228.
108. Juan Ignacio Flores Mogollón, Junta of war, Santa Fe, 23 Feb. 1715, SANM II, 216.
109. Thomas, *After Coronado*, 93.
110. Félix Martínez, Proceedings and campaign journal, Santa Fe and Hopi country, 10 May–20 Nov. 1716, SANM II:250.
111. AASF, DM, 1715:10.
112. Chavez, *Origins*, 216–17
113. Roque Madrid to the Marqués de Valero, Santa Fe, 20 July 1717, AGN Cárceles y presidios, 18.
114. Antonio Valverde Cosío, Notification, 20 Dec. 1717, AGN Cárceles y presidios, 18.
115. Chavez, *Origins*, 216. AASF, DM, 1723:3
116. Stefanie Beninato, "Popé, Pose-yemu, and Naranjo: A New Look at Leadership in the Pueblo Revolt of 1680," NMHR 65 (Oct. 1990): 422–23. For a contemporary Native American historian's view of Naranjo, see Joe S. Sando, *Pueblo Nations: Eight Centuries of Pueblo Indian History* (Santa Fe, 1992), 230–37. Some genealogists challenge the traditional view of Naranjo; they posit that the José Naranjo who was a mulatto and José López Naranjo, an *español* or mestizo, were two different people. See for example, Epifanio Conrado Naranjo, "Naranjo," unpublished manuscript, 1991.
117. Diego de Vargas, Distribution of supplies and livestock, Santa Fe, 1 May 1697, SANM II:65.
118. José Naranjo, Declaration, Halona, 7 Mar. 1702, SANM II:84.
119. Thomas, *After Coronado*, 16, 67.
120. AASF, DM, 1719:16. Chavez, *Origins*, 241–42.
121. Ignacio Flores Mogollón, Junta of war, Santa Fe, 9–12 Aug. 1714, SANM II:209.

122. Thomas, *After Coronado,* 89.
123. Thomas, *After Coronado,* 30, 112.
124. Thomas, *After Coronado,* 38, 187. Antonio Valverde Cosío, Junta of war, Santa Fe, 27 May–3 June 1720, SANM II:308.
125. AASF, DM, 1694:11.
126. AASF, DM, 1712:4.
127. AASF, DM, 1715:14.
128. Antonio Valverde Cosío, Certification, El Paso, 19 Apr. 1701, ZCCL.
129. Francisco Cuervo y Valdés to Juan Roque Gutiérrez, Letter, Santa Fe, 9 May 1706, SANM II:123.
130. Report of goods that Juan Páez Hurtado gave to Francisco Cuervo y Valdés, Santa Fe, 13 Sept. 1707, AGN Vínculos, 125.
131. Myra Ellen Jenkins, "Taos Pueblo and its Neighbors, 1540–1847," NMHR 41 (Apr. 1966): 91, 92.
132. Félix Martínez, Proceedings and campaign journal, Santa Fe and Hopi country, 10 May–20 Nov. 1716, SANM II:250. Ted J. Warner, "Don Félix Martínez and the Santa Fe Presidio, 1693–1730," NMHR 45 (Oct. 1970): 276, 281, 287. BNM 3:1. Reeve, "Navaho-Spanish Wars," 227–29.
133. Juan de Atienza Alcalá to the Marqués de Valero, Santa Cruz, 21 Dec. 1716, AGN Cárceles y presidios, 18.
134. Cristóbal de la Serna, Declaration, Mexico City, 24 Sept. 1717, AGN Cárceles y presidios, 18.
135. Thomas, *After Coronado,* 187.
136. Cristóbal Torres, Petition for land grant, Santa Fe, 1748, SANM I:240. Chavez, *Origins,* 216, 288.
137. Chavez, *Origins,* 291–92.
138. AASF, DM, 1694:18.
139. AASF, DM, 1697:19.
140. Chavez, *Origins,* 291–92.
141. Thomas, *After Coronado,* 88, 91. Reeve, "Navaho-Spanish Wars," 226.
142. Félix Martínez, Proceedings and campaign journal, Santa Fe and Hopi country, 10 May–20 Nov. 1716, SANM II:250.
143. José Rodríguez to Antonio Tafoya, Land sale, Santa Fe, 5 Nov. 1718, SANM I:939.
144. Juan Domingo Bustamante, Order, 20 June 1724, SANM II:516.

145. Juan Páez Hurtado, Criminal investigation, Santa Fe, 18 Jan.–14 May 1735, SANM II:401.
146. Antonio Tafoya, Statement, Santa Fe, 6 Mar. 1745, Univ. of California, Bancroft Library, New Mexico Originals, microfilm collection, r. 1. Reeve, "Navaho-Spanish Wars," 221–22.
147. Antonio Tafoya Altamirano, Will, El Paso, 18 Feb. 1744, SANM I:27. Chavez, *Origins,* 291.
148. Chavez, *Origins,* 108–9.
149. Hackett and Shelby, *Revolt,* 2:103.
150. Chavez, *Origins,* 298. Espinosa, *Crusaders,* 248.
151. AASF, 1696:27.
152. Myra Ellen Jenkins, "Spanish Land Grants in the Tewa Area," NMHR 47 (1972): 120–22.
153. In a deposition about the "limpieza de sangre" of Antonio de los Reyes, who went by Ulibarrí in New Mexico, fray Antonio Pérez de León provided the names of his parents and his birthplace in Michoacán, which is now in the state of Guanajuato. Sacramental records confirm that his parents lived in San Luis de la Paz and that they had a number of other children. There is no baptismal record for Antonio, but there is a gap from 1680 to 1684 in the series of baptisms for this couple, suggesting that they were absent for a time. It seems probable that Antonio was born during this interval. There is also nothing to suggest that Antonio was related to Juan de Ulibarrí, despite several statements to that effect. San Luis de la Paz, Marriages, LDS:0639624 and Burials LDS:0640020. Fray Antonio Pérez de León, Deposition, San Juan Pueblo, 12 Mar. 1727, SANM II:343. Information courtesy of Gerald J. Mandell.
154. Chavez, *Origins,* 299–300.
155. Warner, "Félix Martínez," 272.
156. Thomas, *After Coronado,* 91.
157. Félix Martínez, Proceedings and campaign journal, Santa Fe and Hopi country, 10 May–20 Nov. 1716, SANM II:250.
158. Antonio de Ulibarrí vs. Cristóbal Martín and Antonia de Moraga, Santa Fe, 16 Oct. 1716, SANM I:1021.
159. Antonio de Ulibarrí to María de Tafoya, Land sale, 21 Apr. 1727, SANM I:946.
160. Antonio de Ulibarrí, Land registration, Santa Fe, 20 Jan. 1735, SANM I:1022.

161. Antonio de Ulibarrí, Statement, Santa Fe, 4 Mar. 1745, Univ. of California, Bancroft Library, New Mexico Originals, microfilm collection, r. 1. Reeve, "Navaho-Spanish Wars," 217–18.
162. Chavez, *Origins,* 300.
163. AASF, DM, 1694:24.
164. San Luis Potosí, Baptisms, LDS:0640576.
165. Pedro Rodríguez Cubero, Certification, [Santa Fe], 19 Apr. 1700, ZCCL.
166. Juan de Ulibarrí to Pedro Rodríguez Cubero, Report, Zuni, 8 Mar. 1702, SANM II:85.
167. Ulibarrí's campaign diary is translated in Thomas, *After Coronado,* 59–77.
168. The Marqués de la Peñuela, Order, Santa Fe, 21 Feb. 1709, SANM II:154. The Marqués de la Peñuela, Order, Santa Fe, 8 Dec. 1709, SANM II:157.
169. Juan de Ulibarrí, Petition for a land grant, Santa Fe, 2 Nov. 1709, SANM I:1017.
170. Juan de Ulibarrí, Denunciation of a mine, Santa Fe, 1 Dec. 1709, SANM I:1018.
171. Juan de Ulibarrí, Registration of a mine, Santa Fe, 11 Jan. 1710, SANM I:1019.
172. Juan de Ulibarrí, Investigation, El Paso 6 Nov. 1711, Juárez Municipal Archives (first filming), 1770, r. 45, f. 400.
173. Chavez, *Origins,* 299.
174. Sagrario Metropolitano, Mexico City, Burials, 1714–29, LDS:0035751.
175. Hackett and Shelby, *Revolt,* 2:128.
176. Chavez, *Origins,* 114, 314.
177. Diego de Vargas, Distribution of supplies and livestock, Santa Fe, 1 May 1697, SANM II:65.

Works Cited

Archival Materials
Archive of the Archdiocese of Santa Fe (AASF)
    Diligencias matrimoniales
Archivo General de Indias, Seville (AGI)
    Guadalajara
Archivo General de la Nación, Mexico City (AGN)
    Cárceles y presidios
    Civil
    Historia
    Provincias Internas
    Vínculos
Archivos Históricos del Arzobispado de Durango, Rio Grande Historical Collections, New Mexico State University Library, Las Cruces, New Mexico
The Bancroft Library, University of California, Berkeley, California
    New Mexico Originals
Biblioteca Nacional de México, Archivo Franciscano, Mexico City, Mexico (BNM)
    New Mexico Documents
Biblioteca Nacional de Madrid, Madrid, Spain (BNMad.)
Brigham Young University, Provo, Utah (BYU)
    Spanish New Mexico Collection
The Catholic Archives of Texas, Austin, Texas
    Diligencias matrimoniales
Church of Jesus Christ of Latter-day Saints, Genealogical Library, Salt Lake City, Utah (LDS)
    Microfilm collection of ecclesiastical records, Aguascalientes Mexico City, San Luis de la Paz, San Luis Potosí

Clements Library, University of Michigan, Ann Arbor, Michigan
    Zacatecas Collection (ZCCL)
Juárez Municipal Archives (first filming and second filming), University
    of Texas–El Paso, El Paso, Texas
The Newberry Library, Chicago, Illinois
    Ayer Collection
New Mexico State Records Center and Archives, Santa Fe, New Mexico
    Spanish Archives of New Mexico (SANM) I, II
    Sender Collection
Peabody Museum Library (Rare Book Room, Tozzer Library) Harvard
    University, Cambridge, Massachusetts
    Hemenway Expedition Collections
University of New Mexico, Center for Southwest Research
    Manuscript Collection

OTHER WORKS

Adams, Eleanor B., and Fray Angelico Chavez, eds. and trans. *The Missions of New Mexico, 1776: A Description by Fray Francisco Atanasio Domínguez, with Other Contemporary Documents.* Albuquerque: Univ. of New Mexico Press, 1975.

Amsden, Charles. "Navaho Origins." NMHR 7 (1932): 193–209.

Archibald, Robert. "Acculturation and Assimilation in Colonial New Mexico." NMHR 53 (July 1978): 205–17.

Axtell, James. "The Unkindest Cut, or Who Invented Scalping." In *The European and the Indian: Essays in the Ethnohistory of Colonial North America.* New York: Oxford Univ. Press, 1981.

Bannister, Bryant. *Tree-Ring Dating of the Archeological Sites in the Chaco Canyon Region, New Mexico.* Southwestern Monuments Association Technical Series, 6 (Pt. 2). Globe: Southwestern Monuments Association, 1965.

Bannister, Bryant, William J. Robinson, and Richard L. Warren. *Tree-Ring Dates from New Mexico A, G-H. Shiprock-Zuni-Mt. Taylor Area.* Tucson: Laboratory of Tree-Ring Research, 1970.

Beninato, Stephanie. "Popé, Pose-yemu, and Naranjo: A New Look at Leadership in the Pueblo Revolt of 1680." NMHR 65 (Oct. 1990): 417–35.

Bloom, Lansing B. "A Campaign against the Moqui Pueblos under Governor Phelix Martínez, 1716." NMHR 6 (Apr. 1931): 158–227.

Bolton, Herbert E. *Coronado: Knight of Pueblos and Plains*. Albuquerque: Univ. of New Mexico Press, 1980.

Bover, José M. *María mediadora universal o soteriología mariana estudiada a la luz de principios mariológicos*. Madrid: Consejo Superior de Investigaciones Científicas, 1946.

Brown, Gary M. "Old Wood and Early Navajos: A Chronometric Analysis of the Dinetah Phase." Paper presented at Fifth Annual Navajo Studies Conference, Shiprock, N.M., 1990.

Brown, Gary M., and Patricia M. Hancock. "The Dinetah Phase in the La Plata Valley." In *Cultural Diversity and Adaptation: The Archaic, Anasazi, and Navajo Occupation of the Upper San Juan Basin*. Cultural Resources Series, 9, ed. Lori Stephens Reed and Paul F. Reed. Santa Fe: Bureau of Land Management, 1992.

Brown, Gary M., John A. Evaskovich, Richard G. Holloway, and C. Dean Wilson. *Archaeological Investigations at Grassy Canyon: A Gobernador Phase Navajo Habitation in the Navajo Reservoir District*. Mariah Associates Inc. Technical Report No. 535. Albuquerque: Mariah Associates Inc., 1992.

Brugge, David M. "Discussion of Athabaskan Research." In *Current Research on the Late Prehistory and Early History of New Mexico*. Special Publication, 1, ed. Bradley J. Vierra. Albuquerque: New Mexico Archaeological Council, 1992.

———. "Early 18th-Century Spanish-Apachean Relations." In *Collected Papers in Honor of Bertha Pauline Dutton* (Papers of the Archaeological Society of New Mexico, 4), ed. Albert H. Schroeder. Albuquerque: Albuquerque Archaeological Society Press, 1979.

———. "Eighteenth-Century Fugitives from New Mexico among the Navajos." In *Papers from the Third, Fourth, and Sixth Navajo Studies Conferences*, ed. June-el Piper. Window Rock, Ariz., 1993.

———. "Navajo History." *The Navajo Times*, 9 Sept. 1965, 8B–9B, 23B.

———. "Navajo Prehistory and History to 1850." In *Handbook* 10.

———. "Origin of the Ma'iidesgizhnii Clan." *The Navajo Times*, 9 June 1966, 9.

———. "Origin of the Nakaidene's and Toyahedliinii Clans." *The Navajo Times*, 8 Sept. 1966, 29B.

Burrus, Ernest J., S.J. *Kino and Manje: Explorers of Sonora and Arizona*. Rome: Jesuit Historical Institute, 1971.

———. "A Tragic Interlude in the Reconquest of New Mexico." *Manuscripta* 29 (Nov. 1985): 154–65.

Carlson, Roy L. *Eighteenth Century Navajo Fortresses of the Gobernador District.* University of Colorado Series in Anthropology, 10. Boulder: Univ. of Colorado Press, 1965.

Carol, Juniper B., ed., *Mariology.* 3 vols. Milwaukee: Bruce Publishing, 1961.

Casado Fuente, Ovidio. *Don Francisco Cuerbo y Valdés, governador de Nuevo México, fundador de la ciudad de Alburquerque.* Oviedo: Instituto de Estudios Asturianos, 1983.

Chavez, Fray Angelico, O.F.M. *Archives of the Archdiocese of Santa Fe, 1678–1900.* Publications of the Academy of American Franciscan History, Bibliographical Series, 3. Washington, D.C.: Academy of American Franciscan History, 1957.

———. *The Origins of New Mexico Families in the Spanish Colonial Period in Two Parts: The Seventeenth (1598–1693), and the Eighteenth (1693–1821) Centuries,* 1954. Reprint, Santa Fe: William Gannon, 1975.

———. "Genízaros." In *Handbook* 9.

Collins, Roger. *Early Medieval Spain: Unity in Diversity, 400–1000.* New York: St. Martin's Press, 1983.

Correll, J. Lee. "Events in Navajo History No. 18. Navajo-Ute Relations Prior to the 1870s and Naahoondzho—'The Fearing Time'." *The Navajo Times,* 26 Jan. 1967, 10–11.

Cutter, Charles, R. *The Protector de Indios in Colonial New Mexico, 1659–1821.* Albuquerque: Univ. of New Mexico Press, 1986.

Dittert, Jr. Alfred E. "Salvage Archaeology and the Navajo Project: A Progress Report." *El Palacio* 65 (1958): 61–72.

Dozier, Edward P. *The Pueblo Indians of North America.* New York: Holt, Rinehart and Winston, Inc., 1970.

Enciclopedia universal ilustrada europeo-americana. 70 vols. Barcelona: Hijos de J. Espasa, ed., 1907–30.

Espinosa, J. Manuel. *Crusaders of the Río Grande: The Story of Don Diego de Vargas and the Reconquest and Refounding of New Mexico.* 1942. Reprint, Salisbury, N.C.: Documentary Publications, 1977.

——— ed. and trans. *The Pueblo Indian Revolt of 1696 and the Franciscan Missions of New Mexico: Letters of the Missionaries and Related Documents.* Norman: Univ. of Oklahoma Press, 1988.

———. "The Virgin of the Reconquest of New Mexico." *Mid-America: An Historical Review* 18 (Apr. 1936): 79–87.

Flagler, Edward K. "Defensive Policy and Indian Relations in New Mexico during the Tenure of Governor Francisco Cuervo y Valdés, 1705–1707." *Revista Española de Antropología Americana* 22 (1992): 89–104.

———. "Governor José Chacón, Marqués de la Peñuela: An Andalusian Nobleman on the New Mexico Frontier. NMHR 65 (Oct 1990): 455–75.

Forbes, Jack D. *Apache, Navaho, and Spaniard.* Norman: Univ. of Oklahoma Press, 1960.

Frazer, Robert W. "The Battle of Cienguilla." *La Crónica de Nuevo Mexico* 9 (Santa Fe, 1980): 3–5.

Glover, Charles. "Classification of Irrigation Water." *New Mexico State University Cooperative Extension Service Guide A-110.* Las Cruces: New Mexico State Univ., 1984.

Gunnerson, James H. "Plateau Shoshonean Prehistory: A Suggested Reconstruction." *American Antiquity* 28 (1962): 41–45.

Hackett, Charles Wilson, ed. *Historical Documents Relating to New Mexico, Nueva Vizcaya, and Approaches Thereto to 1773.* 3 vols. Washington, D. C.: Carnegie Institution of Washington, 1923–37.

Hackett, Charles Wilson, and Charmion Clair Shelby, trans. *Revolt of the Pueblo Indians of New Mexico and Otermín's Attempted Reconquest, 1680–1682.* 2 vols. Coronado Cuarto Centennial Publications, 1540–1940, 8–9. Albuquerque: Univ. of New Mexico Press, 1942.

Hammond, George P., and Agapito Rey, *Don Juan de Oñate, Colonizer of New Mexico, 1595–1628.* 2 vols. Albuquerque: Univ. of New Mexico Press, 1953.

Hancock, Patricia M. "Evidence of the Dinetah Phase in the La Plata River Valley, San Juan County, New Mexico." In *Current Research on the Late Prehistory and Early History of New Mexico.* Special Publication, 1, ed. Bradley J. Vierra. Albuquerque, 1992.

Handbook. See Ortiz, Alfonso, ed.

Hester, James J. *Early Navajo Migrations and Acculturation in the Southwest.* Museum of New Mexico Papers in Anthropology, 6. Santa Fe: 1962.

Hill, W. W. "Some Navaho Culture Changes during Two Centuries (with a Translation of the Early Eighteenth Century Rabal Manuscript)." In *Essays in Historical Anthropology of North America.* Smithsonian Miscellaneous Collections, vol. 100. Washington, D.C.: Smithsonian Institution, 1940.

Hodge, Frederick Webb. "The Early Navaho and Apache." *American Anthropologist* 8 (o.s.)(1895): 223–40.

Hogan, Patrick. "Dinetah: A Reevaluation of Pre-Revolt Navajo Occupation in Northwest New Mexico." *Journal of Anthropological Research* 45 (1989): 53–66.

———. "Navajo-Pueblo Interaction during the Gobernador Phase: A Reassessment of the Evidence." In *Rethinking Navajo Pueblitos*. Cultural Resources Series, 8, contributors Michael P. Marshall and Patrick Hogan. Farmington, N.M.: Bureau of Land Management, 1991.

Jacobson, LouAnn, Stephen Fosberg, and Robert Bewley. "Navajo Defensive Systems in the Eighteenth Century." In *Cultural Diversity and Adaptation: The Archaic, Anasazi, and Navajo Occupation of the Upper San Juan Basin*. Cultural Resources Series, 9, ed. Lori Stephens Reed and Paul F. Reed. Santa Fe: Bureau of Land Management, 1992.

Jenkins, Myra Ellen. "Spanish Land Grants in the Tewa Area," NMHR 47 (1972): 120–22.

——— "Taos Pueblo and its Neighbors, 1540–1847." NMHR 41 (Apr. 1966): 85–114.

John, Elizabeth A. H. *Storms Brewed in Other Men's Worlds: The Confrontation of Indians, Spanish, and French in the Southwest, 1540–1795*. Bison Books. Lincoln: Univ. of Nebraska, 1981.

Jones, Oakah L., Jr. *Nueva Vizcaya: Heartland of the Spanish Frontier*. Albuquerque: Univ. of New Mexico Press, 1988.

———. *Pueblo Warriors and Spanish Conquest*. Norman: Univ. of Oklahoma Press, 1966.

Kessell, John L., and Rick Hendricks, eds. *By Force of Arms: The Journals of don Diego de Vargas, New Mexico, 1691–1693*. Albuquerque: Univ. of New Mexico Press, 1992.

Kessell, John L., Rick Hendricks, and Meredith D. Dodge, eds. *To the Royal Crown Restored: The Journals of don Diego de Vargas, 1692–94*. Albuquerque: Univ. of New Mexico Press, 1995.

Kidder, Alfred V. "Ruins of the Historic Period in the Upper San Juan Valley, New Mexico." *American Anthropologist* 22 (1920): 322–29.

Kluckhohn, Clyde, and Dorothea Leighton. *The Navajo*. Cambridge, Mass.: Harvard Univ. Press, 1960.

Lange, Charles H. *Cochiti: A New Mexico Pueblo, Past and Present.* Austin: Univ. of Texas Press, 1959.

Ligon, J. Stokley. *New Mexico Birds and Where to Find Them.* Albuquerque: Univ. of New Mexico Press, in cooperation with the New Mexico Department of Game and Fish, 1961.

The Liturgy of the Hours According to the Roman Rite. New York: Catholic Book Publishing, 1975.

Marshall, Michael P. *The Excavation of the Cortez CO2 Pipeline Project Sites, 1982–1983.* Univ. of New Mexico Office of Contract Archeology. Albuquerque: Office of Contract Archeology, 1985.

———. "The Pueblito as a Site Complex: Archeological Investigations in the Dinetah District." In *Rethinking Navajo Pueblitos.* Cultural Resources Series, 8, contributors Michael P. Marshall and Patrick Hogan. Farmington, N.M.: Bureau of Land Management, 1991.

McNitt, Frank. *Navajo Wars: Military Campaigns, Slave Raids, and Reprisals.* Albuquerque: Univ. of New Mexico Press, 1972.

Milich, Alicia Ronstadt, trans. *Relaciones by Zárate Salmerón.* Albuquerque: Univ. of New Mexico Press, 1966.

Morrison, Chas. C. "Executive and Descriptive Report of Lieutenant C. C. Morrison, Sixth Cavalry, on the Operations of Party No. 2, Colorado Section, Field-Season of 1875," Appendix E to Appendix JJ, George M. Wheeler, Annual Report, Geographical Surveys West of the 100th Meridian. In *Annual Report of the Chief of Engineers for 1876.* 44th Cong. 2d Sess. HED 1, Pt. 2 (Serial No. 1745), 356–67. Washington, D.C.: U.S. Government Printing Office, 1876.

Naranjo, Epifanio Conrado. "Naranjo." Unpublished manuscript in authors' possession, 1991.

Navarro García, Luis. *Sonora y Sinaloa en el siglo xvii.* Seville: Escuela de Estudios Hispano-Americanos, 1967.

Naylor, Thomas H., and Charles W. Polzer, S.J., comps. and eds. *The Presidio and Militia on the Northern Frontier of New Spain: A Documentary History, 1570–1700.* Vol. 1. Tucson: Univ. of Arizona Press, 1986.

New Mexico Office of Cultural Affairs, Historic Preservation Division, Archeological Records Management System, LA 8948 site files. Santa Fe, 1971.

New Mexico State University Soil, Water, and Plant Testing Laboratory. "Water Analysis Report, Lab. No. 7156, 6 June 1988." Las Cruces, 1988.

Opler, Morris E. "The Apachean Culture Pattern and Its Origins." In *Handbook* 10.

Ortiz, Alfonso, ed. *Southwest.* Vols. 9 and 10 of *Handbook of North American Indians.* Washington, D.C.: Smithsonian Institution, 1983.

Parmentier, Richard J. "The Pueblo Mythological Triangle: Poseyemu, Montezuma, and Jesus in the Pueblos." In *Handbook* 9.

Pearce, T. M. *New Mexico Place Names.* Albuquerque: Univ. of New Mexico Press, 1965.

Perry, Richard J. "The Apachean Transition from the Subarctic to the Southwest" *Plains Anthropologist,* 25(90)(1980): 279–96.

———. *Western Apache Heritage: People of the Mountain Corridor.* Austin: Univ. of Texas Press, 1991.

Peterson, Harold L. *Arms and Armor in Colonial America, 1526–1783.* New York: Bramhall House, 1956.

Powers, Margaret A., and Byron P. Johnson, *Defensive Sites of Dinetah,* Cultural Resources Series, 2. Albuquerque: Bureau of Land Management, 1987.

Reed, Alan D., and Jonathan C. Horn, "Early Navajo Occupation of the American Southwest: Reexamination of the Dinetah Phase." *Kiva* 55 (1990): 293.

Reed, Alan D., Patricia M. Hancock, Timothy M. Kearns, Margaret A. Powers, and Roger A. Moore. *Excavations at Three Early Navajo Sites in the La Plata Valley.* Division of Conservation Archaeology Studies in Archaeology, 7. Farmington, N.M.: San Juan County Museum Association, 1988.

Reed, Lori Stephens, and Paul F. Reed, "The Protohistoric Navajo: Implications of Interaction, Exchange, and Alliance Formation with the Eastern and Western Pueblos." In *Cultural Diversity and Adaptation: The Archaic, Anasazi, and Navajo Occupation of the Upper San Juan Basin.* Cultural Resources Series, 9, ed. Lori Stephens Reed and Paul F. Reed. Santa Fe: Bureau of Land Management, 1992.

Reeve, Frank D. "Early Navaho Geography." NMHR 31 (1956): 290–309.

———. "The Navaho-Spanish Peace: 1720's–1770's," NMHR 34 (1959): 9–40.

———. "Navaho-Spanish Wars, 1680–1720." NMHR 33 (1958): 205–31.

———. "Seventeenth Century Navaho-Spanish Relations." NMHR 32 (1957): 36–52.

Robinson, William J., Bruce G. Harrill, and Richard L. Warren. *Tree-Ring Dates from New Mexico B. Chaco-Gobernador Area.* Tucson: Labratory of Tree-Ring Research, 1974.

Sando, Joe S. *Pueblo Nations: Eight Centuries of Pueblo Indian History.* Santa Fe: Clear Light Publishers, 1992.

Santamaría, Francisco J. *Diccionario de mejicanismos.* Mexico City: Editorial Porrúa, 1983.

Schaafsma, Curtis F. "A Review of the Documentary Evidence for a Seventeenth-Century Navajo Occupation in the Chama Valley." In *Current Research on the Late Prehistory and Early History of New Mexico.* Special Publication, 1, ed. Bradley J. Vierra. Albuquerque: New Mexico Archaeological Council, 1992.

Schroeder, Albert H. "A Brief History of the Southern Utes." *Southwestern Lore* 30 (1965): 53–78.

Simmons, Marc. "Settlement Patterns and Village Plans in Colonial New Mexico." In *New Spain's Far Northern Frontier: Essays on Spain in the American West, 1540–1821,* ed. David J. Weber. Albuquerque: Univ. of New Mexico Press, 1979.

Spaulding, Robert K. *How Spanish Grew.* Berkeley: Univ. of California Press, 1943.

Stahlecker, Dale, and Martin Frentzel. *Seasons of the Crane.* Albuquerque: Heritage Associates, 1986.

Stephen, Alexander M. *Hopi Journal of Alexander M. Stephen.* Columbia University Contributions to Anthropology, vol. 2, ed. Elsie C. Parsons. Reprint, New York: AMS Press, 1969.

Strong, Pauline Turner. "Santa Ana Pueblo." In *Handbook* 9.

Strout, Clevy Lloyd. "The Resettlement of Santa Fe, 1695: The Newly Found Muster Roll." 53 (July 1978): 261–70.

Tedlock, Dennis. "Zuni Religion and World View." In *Handbook* 9.

Thomas, Alfred Barnaby. *After Coronado: Spanish Exploration Northeast of New Mexico, 1696–1727.* Norman: Univ. of Oklahoma Press, 1935.

Tiller, Veronica E. Velarde. *The Jicarilla Apache Tribe: A History, 1846–1970.* Lincoln: Univ. of Nebraska, 1983.

Towner, Ronald H., and Jeffrey S. Dean. "LA 2298: The Oldest Pueblito Revisited." *Kiva* 57 (1992): 315–29.

Vargas Machuca, Bernardo de. *Milicia y descripción de las Indias.* 1599. 2 vols. Reprint, Madrid: Librería de Victoriano Suárez, 1892.

Vargas Ugarte, Rubén., S.J. *Historia del culto de María en Iberoamérica y de sus imágenes y santuarios más celebrados.* 3d ed. Madrid: Talleres Gráficos Jura, 1956.

Warner, Ted J. "Don Félix Martínez and the Santa Fe Presidio, 1693–1730." NMHR 45 (Oct. 1970): 269–310.

White, Leslie A. *The Acoma Indians: People of the Sky City.* 47th Annual Report of the Bureau of American Ethnology. Washington, D.C.: U.S. Government Printing Office, 1932.

Wilcox, David R. "The Entry of Athapaskans into the American Southwest: The Problem Today." In *The Protohistoric Period in the North American Southwest, A.D. 1450–1700,* ed. David R. Wilcox and W. Bruce Masse. Arizona State University Anthropological Research Papers, 24. Tempe: Arizona State Univ. 1981.

Wilson, John P., and A. H. Warren, "LA 2298, The Earliest Pueblito?" *Awanyu* 2:1 (1974): 8–26.

Winter, Joseph C., and Patrick Hogan, "The Dinetah Phase of Northwestern New Mexico: Settlement and Subsistence." In *Current Research on the Late Prehistory and Early History of New Mexico.* Special Publication, 1, ed. Bradley J. Vierra. Albuquerque: New Mexico Archaeological Council, 1992.

Wiseman, Regge N. *An Archaeological Clearance Investigation and Impact Statement of Two Southern Union Gas Company Cathodic Protection Lines South of Gobernador, New Mexico.* Museum of New Mexico Laboratory of Anthropology Note No. 122. Santa Fe: Museum of New Mexico, 1975.

Worcester, Donald E. "The Navaho during the Spanish Regime in New Mexico." NMHR, 26 (1951): 101–18.

Wozniak, Frank E. "The Location of the Navajo Homeland in the Seventeenth Century: An Appraisal of the Spanish Colonial Records." In *Current Research on the Late Prehistory and Early History of New Mexico.* Special Publication, 1, ed. Bradley J. Vierra. Albuquerque: New Mexico Archaeological Council, 1992.

Wright, Gary A. "The Shoshonean Migration Problem." *Plains Anthropologist* 23 (80)(1978): 113–37.

Young, Robert W. "Apachean Languages." In *Handbook* 10.

Index

Abiquiu, N.M. 90, 123, 146 n3
Acoma Pueblo 96, 102, 120, 138 n2; alcalde of 125; battle of (1599) 7, 144 n18; milpas in Navajo country 37, 61, 94; presidial troops at 3
Adams, Eleanor B. 131 n1, 138 n2
Agua Caliente Canyon 66
Albert Canyon 84
Albert Mesa 82, 84
Albuquerque 96, 106, 125, 127
Alburquerque, Duque de (Francisco Fernández de la Cueva Enríquez) 91, 96, 97, 121
Alvarez Castrillón, Antonio 37, 38, 60, 61, 148 n2; biographical sketch of 101
Alvarez Castrillón, Pedro 148 n2
Anaya, Juan de 125
Apaches 1, 3, 66, 96, 110, 113, 115, 117, 123, 127, 146 n4 *see also* specific groups, such as Jicarilla
Archuleta, Antonia 109
Archuleta, Micaela 109
Arellano, Cristóbal de 37, 59, 104; biographical sketch of 102–3
Arellano, Nicolás de 102
Argüello, Juana de 124
Armijo, Rosa 124
Arvid [Arvizu y Gamboa], Juana de 117, 120
Avalos, Antonio 109
Ayeta, fray Francisco de 139 n5

Bandelier, Adolph xi, xvi, xviii, xix, 144
Bandelier, Adolphe Eugene xviii, 144
Bernalillo 2, 27, 52, 96, 103, 107, 109
Blanco Wash 7
Boulder Lake 68, 69
Briggs Mesa 69
Burns Canyon 73, 74
Burns Hill 71
Bustamante, Gov. Juan Domingo de 123

Cañada de Tío Roques 69
Candelaria, Francisco de la Luz 106
Cañon Largo xviii, 78, 82, 84, 86, 87, 93
Carlanas Apaches 96
Carracas Mesa 71
Casa fuerte 68, 137 n2
Castellanos, José de 125
Cereza Canyon xviii, 69, 82, 93
Chama, N.M. xix, xx, 64, 67, 96
Chama River 19, 44, 67, 139 n3
Chama Valley 69, 99
Chillo, Juan 115
Cisneros Canyon 69
Cochiti Pueblo 3, 96, 105, 113, 115, 128
Codallos y Rabal, Gov. Joaquín 6

169

Colina, fray Agustín de 34, 57; biographical sketch of 103
Comanches 6, 93, 96, 100, 121, 132 n15
Compañero Arroyo 69
Copper Hill 66
Cotton 96, 147 n15
Cruz, María de la 110
Cruzat y Góngora, Gov. Gervasio 123
Cuba, N.M. 87
Cuencamé, presidio at 101, 122
Cuervo y Valdés, Gov. Francisco 1–4, 13, 39, 121, 122, 125; Indian policy of 94–98, 103; reports on Navajo campaigns by xx, 91–92

Davidson, 1st. Lt. John 66
Dirucaca (Governor of Picuris Pueblo) 19, 44, 68; biographical sketch of 103–4
Domínguez, fray Francisco Atanasio 65, 66
Domínguez, Juan Antonio 105
Domínguez de Mendoza, Antonio 104
Domínguez de Mendoza, Joseph 37, 59; biographical sketch of 104–5
Domínguez de Mendoza, Juan 113, 137 n2
Dulce, N.M. 68, 69, 70, 71, 73
Dulce Canyon 71
Dulce Lake 71
Durán, Josefa 117, 121
Durán y Chaves, María 124

El Cuartelejo 97, 112, 120, 127
El Embudo 13, 39
El Paso 103, 104, 114, 124, 125, 141 n7; alcalde of 127; presidio of 105, 107, 109, 113, 116, 121, 127–28
Embudo Creek 65

Embudo Pass 65
Enbom Lake 68
Enchanted Mesa 118
Enríquez de los Reyes, José 124
Ensenada Mesa 82
Española, N.M. 65, 120

Faraón Apaches 1, 96, 117
Fernández, Alonso 137 n2
Fernández de Valus Bercerra, Leonor 102
Flores Mogollón, Gov. Ignacio 99, 100, 101, 104, 110, 111, 117, 118, 121, 122
Franciscans, activity among Navajos of 6, 133 n18

Gallegos, Diego 107
Gallegos, José 107
Gallegos Canyon 7
García, Juan 107
García, María 107
García, Mariana 109
García, Martín 37, 59; biographical sketch of 106
García de Noriega, Alonso II 122
Genízaros 19, 20, 30, 44, 54, 69, 94, 140 n7
Gila Apaches 1, 3
Gila River Pimas 93
Girón, Tomás 141 n8
Godines, María Luisa 122
Gómez, Antonio 109
Gómez, Ursula 110
González Castrillón, José 101
Griego, Agustin 117, 121
Griego, Blas 106
Griego, Josefa 106
Griego, Juan 32, 56; biographical sketch of 106
Griego, Juan (Tewa leader) 106, 115
Griego, Lorenzo 121
Guillén, Pedro 105

Gutiérrez, Alejo 18, 43;
  biographical sketch of 106–7
Gutiérrez, Juan Roque 70;
  biographical sketch of 107–9;
  on 1705 expedition 18, 19, 21,
  26, 30, 37, 38, 43, 44, 46, 50, 55,
  59, 61
Gutiérrez, Roque 106, 107

Halona 118
Herrera, Juan de 109, 137 n2
Herrera, María de 109
Herrera, Miguel de 25, 37, 49, 59;
  biographical sketch of 109
Hinojos, María de 124
Hinojosa, fray Joaquín de 103
Hodge, Frederick Webb 8
Holguín *see* López Holguín
Holy Ghost Spring 38, 61, 85, 86–87
Hopi 96, 108, 109, 117, 141 n9, 143
  n16; Governor Martínez's 1716
  campaign against 103, 105, 110,
  117, 121, 123, 125; Pueblo
  refugees at 91–92
Horses 16, 18, 24, 25, 28, 51, 54, 71,
  82, 105, 108, 121, 132 n15, 138 n2
Hurtado, Catarina 107
Hurtado, María 107

Inscription Rock (El Morro) 120,
  127

Jauguada de Ulloa, Felipa 122
Jemez Pueblo 19, 20, 44, 45, 96;
  alcalde of 103; genízaros at 19,
  20, 44, 69, 94; Navajo attack on
  98–99; presidial troops at 3;
  refugees among Navajos 20, 45,
  90, 92
Jicarilla Apaches 66, 146 n4
Jiménez, fray Francisco 14, 40;
  biographical sketch of 112
Jironza Petrís de Cruzate, Gov.
  Domingo 104, 105, 113, 114

K'iakima 91

LA 2298 xix, 6, 85–86, 93;
  photograph of 85
LA 8948 xix, 79
LA 61838 8
La Cieneguilla 13, 39, 66
La Fragua Canyon 76
Laguna de San Joseph xix, 24, 28,
  47, 48, 53, 63, 71, 72, 73, 74, 81;
  photograph of 23, 73
Laguna Pueblo 96, 98, 120; alcalde
  of 125; establishment of 118;
  milpas in Navajo country 37, 61,
  94; presidial troops at 3
Laguna Seca 71
La Jara Canyon xxi, 69, 76, 77, 81,
  93, 94; photograph of 25, 50
La Jara Mesa 71
La Jara Spring 69
La Mesita 65
La Sierrita 66
La Vega 120
Leyba, Juana de 110
Llaves, N.M. 68
Lobato, Bartolomé 102–3
López, Juana 104
López [del Castillo], Ana 109
López Holguín, Antonio 110
López Holguín, Juan 109
López Holguín, Tomás 37, 59, 117,
  118; biographical sketch of
  109–12,
Los Pedernales 90, 123, 146 n3
Los Peñoles 64, 68, 69, 78, 81, 93,
  126, 138 n2, 146 n3; in 1705
  campaign journal 19, 26, 27, 28,
  29, 30, 44, 50, 51, 53, 55;
  photograph of 52 *see also*
  Magdalena Butte and Santos
  Peak
Luján, Antonia 109
Luján, Catalina 120
Luján, Cristóbal 124

Luján, Juan 105
Luján, María 109
Luján, Matías 120

[Madrid], Antonia 117
Madrid, Francisco, II 112
Madrid, José 117
Madrid, Josefa 117, 120
[Madrid], Julián 117
Madrid, Lorenzo 112
Madrid, Matías 117, 121
[Madrid], Miguel Angel 117
Madrid, Pedro 117, 121
Madrid, Roque xv, xvi, xxi, 4–5, 6, 92, 101, 111, 120–21; biographical sketch of 112–18; on 1705 expedition 13, 36, 37, 38, 39, 59, 60, 61, 63; reconstructed route of 65–69, 71, 74, 81, 82, 84, 86, 87 subsequent campaigns of 98, 99, 120
Maese, Catalina 105
Magdalena Butte 68, 77, 81 *see also* Los Peñoles
Manje, Juan Mateo 93
Mariquita, Cristóbal (Tewa leader) 121
Márquez, Antonio 106
Márquez, Diego 120
Márquez, Juana 120
Márquez, Margarita 107
Martín, Alejo 121
Martín, Antonia 107
Martín, Blas 92
Martín, Cristóbal 125
Martín, Micaela 124
Martín, Nicolás Jacinto 121
Martín, Pedro 124
Martínez, Félix 1716 Hopi campaign of 103, 105, 110, 117, 125; struggle with Governor Flores Mogollón 111, 118, 121, 122
Matthews, Washington 8

McNitt, Frank xviii, xxii
Miera y Pacheco, Bernardo de 66, 67
Milpas, location of xv, 24, 30, 47, 49, 54, 55, 76, 82, 94
Mirabal, Carlos de 123
Mizquía, Francisca de 128
Monero, N.M. 69
Mora, Juan de la *see* Zamora
Moraga, Alonso de 110
Moraga, Antonia de 125
Moraga, Micaela de 110
Morrison, Lt. C.C 86
Mules 2, 104, 105, 112, 115, 125
Muñoz Canyon xxii, 8, 93

Naranjo, José [López] 31, 37, 56, 60, 98, 154 n116; biographical sketch of 118, 120; painting of 119
Naranjo, José Antonio 120
Navajo River 21, 46–47, 68–69, 70, 71; photograph of 46
Navajos, agricultural techniques of 76, 89–90, 93; battles with Madrid's forces 24–25, 28–33, 49, 50–54, 63, 64, 65, 81, 84, 86; leaders xx, 95, 96; pottery 8, 9, 79; Pueblo refugees among 6, 7, 20, 90–93; settlement patterns of 3, 20, 21, 23, 25, 26, 30, 37, 44, 45, 47, 49, 50, 51, 54, 61, 90, 95, 96; territory of, 6–9, 68–74, 75–79, 81–82 84–87, 94, 96; weapons 25, 49
New Biscay 1, 3, 101, 114
Nuestra Señora de Covadonga 16, 41, 136 n1
Nuestra Señora de la Conquista 16, 18, 43, 139 n6

Ojeda, Gertrudis Josefa de 128
Ojo de Espíritu Santo *see* Holy Ghost Spring

Ojo de Nuestra Señora de Guadalupe (campsite) see Otero Ranch Spring
Otermín, Gov. Antonio de 104, 113, 118, 128, 137 n2
Otero Ranch Spring 34, 57, 58, 65, 85, 86–87; photograph of 36

Páez Hurtado, Juan 102, 117, 120, 122, 123, 125
Palacios, María de 120
Pamuje 19, 44, 68, 141 n8
Pecos 103, 114, 120
Peñuela, Marqués de la (José Chacón Medina Salazar y Villaseñor) 98, 99, 116, 120, 121
Pérez de León, fray Antonio 156 n153
Perlaja xx, 95, 96
Picuris Pueblo 13, 39, 65, 66, 94, 96, 98, 115, 120, 125, 126; governor of 103–4; refugees returned from El Cuartelejo to 97, 112, 127; war captain from 16, 41, 63
Piedra del Carnero 15, 40, 66 see also Tres Piedras
Piedra Lumbre 96, 99, 137 n2
Pilar, N.M. 66; photograph of 14 see also La Cieneguilla
Pojoaque Pueblo 97, 120
Pueblitos 6, 7, 85, 86, 93 see also torreones
Pueblo revolt, of 1680 9, 91–92, 96, 104, 112, 118, 139 n5; of 1696 6, 91–92, 115, 118, 124, 127, 128, 141 n8

Rael de Aguilar, Alfonso 94, 117
Rael de Aguilar, Teresa Antonia 125
Ramos, Josefa see Reinoso
Ramos de Arellano, Ursula see Reinoso

Reeve, Frank xviii, 147 n15
Reinoso, Josefa 102
Reinoso, Ursula 102
Rendón, Francisco 105
Reneros de Posada, Gov. Pedro 105, 114
Río de las Grullas 18, 43, 67
Río de los Pinos 67
Río del Norte see also Rio Grande 13, 15, 19, 21, 39, 40, 44, 47, 65
Río Grande 64, 65, 66, 69, 117
Río Grande see also San Juan River 19, 20, 21, 24, 27, 35, 44, 45, 46, 49, 52, 58, 68, 69, 96
Río Tusas 67
Rito Cieneguilla 66
Rocha, María de la 121
Rodríguez Cubero, Gov. Pedro xv, 1, 102, 103, 115, 118, 127, 146 n4
Romero, Alonso 124
Romero, Graciana 102
Romero, Inés 106
Romero, José 106
Ruiz de Cáceres, Sebastiana 112
Ruiz de Esparza, Leonor see Fernández de Valus Bercerra

Sáiz, Agustín 106
Sáiz, Juliana 106
San Ildefonso Pueblo 96, 98, 103, 110, 120, 124; Navajo attack on 1, 94–95
San Juan Mountains 67, 139 n3
San Juan Pueblo xviii, 5, 67, 98, 99, 106, 120; complaint against Madrid by 116; Navajo attack on 1, 94–95
San Juan River 7, 8, 9, 68, 69, 70, 71, 76, 96, 137 n2
Sánchez, Pedro 6
Sangre de Cristo Mountains 139 n3
San Lorenzo 104, 106
San Miguel Arcangel mine 127

Santa Clara Pueblo 96, 98, 120, 123, 124, 141 n8; Navajo attack on 1, 94–95, 116; presidial troops at 3, 5
Santa Cruz, N.M. 2, 89, 99, 105, 109, 115, 118; alcalde of 103, 110, 116, 127; plan to abandon 117; resettlement of 97
Santa Fe, alcalde of 94, 108, 125; archives at xviii, xix, 91; cabildo of 90, 92, 95; presidio of 2–3, 101, 102, 106, 109, 117, 118, 121, 122, 125
Santa María de Grado 97
Santa Rosa mine 127
Santos Peak xviii, xxi, 68, 77, 78, 81; photograph of 29, 78, 79 *see also* Los Peñoles
Scalping 28, 53, 99, 142 n16
Scholes, France V. 138 n2
Serna, Antonia de la 121
Serna, Cristóbal de la 37, 60, 99–100, 111, 117; biographical sketch of 120–22
Serna, Felipe de la 120
Serna, Isabel de la 121
Serna, Juan de la 121
Serna, María de la 120
Serna, Sebastián de la 121
Serna, Sebastiana de la 121
Sheep 27, 31, 66, 93, 96, 115, 126
Sierra de las Grullas 18, 42, 43, 67, 89, 123, 139 n4, 146 n3
Sierra Florida 15, 16, 41, 67; photograph of 41
Socorro, Tex. 103, 110, 113
Solá Cubero, Miguel 102
Stinking Lake 68, 69
Stock Driveway Canyon 69
Suicide 33, 57, 143 n18

Tafoya Altamirano, Antonio 89, 128, 146 n3; biographical sketch of 122–24

Tafoya Altamirano de Estrada, Juan de 122
Tafoya, María de 125
Tagle, fray Juan de 89, 91
Taos Pueblo 14, 40, 94, 96, 112, 118, 120; participants in 1705 expedition 14, 40, 66
Tapia, María de 106, 107, 124
Tapicito Creek 82, 84, 94
Tapicito Ruin *see* LA 2298 85
Téllez Girón, José 107
Tesuque Pueblo 13, 39, 97, 103, 120
Tlalpujahua 122, 128
Toltec Gorge 67
Torreones 7, 99, 148 n26 *see also* pueblito
Torres, Cristóbal 122
Tree-ring dates 6, 7, 8, 79, 85
Tres Piedras xix, 66, 67 *see also* Piedra del Carnero
Treviño, Gov. Juan Francisco 104, 137 n2
Truby Ranch 84
Trujillo, Cristóbal 109
Trujillo, Diego 109
Trujillo, José 89–90, 98, 99, 109
Trujillo, Mateo 27, 37, 51, 60; biographical sketch of 124
Trujillo, Miguel 109
Tuckers Ridge 69

Ulibarrí, Antonio de 156 n153; biographical sketch of 124–26
Ulibarrí, Feliciana de 125
Ulibarrí, José de 126
Ulibarrí, Juan de 13, 39, 97, 118, 120, 124, 125, 126; biographical sketch of 126–28
Ulibarrí, María de 126
Utes 7, 9, 93, 96, 100, 121

Valdés, Juan Lorenzo de 123
Valle de Santiago 16, 18, 42, 67

Valverde Cosío, Gov. Antonio 111, 116, 118, 122, 128, 132 n15
Vaqueros Canyon 74, 76; photograph of 77
Varela, Antonia 106
Varela de Perea, Gerónima 105
Vargas, Gov. Diego de 1, 3, 65, 102, 103, 107, 114, 115, 116, 118, 122, 128, 139 n6, 142 n12
Vega, María de la 128
Vegetation, flowers 15, 40; bushes 15, 21, 24, 40, 46, 47, 76; quelites 20, 45; trees 19, 44
Velarde, N.M. 65
Velasco, Diego 109
Vélez de Escalante, fray Silvertre xviii, 91, 145 n1
Villasur expedition 105, 111, 120, 122

Walpi 108, 111
Warren, Mrs. A.H. 79
Weapons, firearms 2, 18, 43, 105, 139 n5
Wheeler Survey 64, 65, 66, 86

Wildlife, birds 16, 18, 42, 138 n3, 139 n4; deer 20, 45; fish 18, 43
Willow Creek 69
Wiseman, Regge xxii
Wozniak, Frank xix, xxi

Ysleta, Tex. 106, 113

[Zamora], Antonio 128
[Zamora], Josefa 128
Zamora, Juan de 18, 43; biographical sketch of 128
[Zamora], María 128
Zárate Salmerón, fray Gerónimo de 9
Zia Pueblo xviii, 31, 61, 64, 96, 103, 109, 126, 137 n2, 146 n3; alcalde of 103; 1705 expedition at 38, 56, 87
Zuni Pueblo 3, 94, 96, 98, 120, 125; alcalde of 125; presidial soldiers at 3, 102, 108, 109; Pueblo refugees at 91–92

www.ingramcontent.com/pod-product-compliance
Lightning Source LLC
Chambersburg PA
CBHW021842220426
43663CB00005B/365